Mary 101

Mark McVann, FSC

Mary 101
Tradition and Influence

MARY ANN ZIMMER, ND, PhD

Liguori
ONE LIGUORI DRIVE
LIGUORI MO 63057-9999

Imprimi Potest:
Thomas D. Picton, C.Ss.R.
Provincial, Denver Province
The Redemptorists

Published by Liguori Publications
Liguori, Missouri
To order, call 800-325-9521
www.liguori.org

Library of Congress Cataloging-in-Publication Data

Zimmer, Mary Ann, 1946-
    Mary 101 : tradition and influence / Mary Ann Zimmer.
        p. cm.
    ISBN 978-0-7648-1851-6
    1. Mary, Blessed Virgin, Saint. I. Title.
    BT603.Z56 2010
    232.91—dc22

                      2010000365

Liguori Publications, a nonprofit corporation, is an apostolate of the Redemptorists. To learn more about the Redemptorists, visit Redemptorists.com.

Printed in the United States of America
14 13 12 11 10   5 4 3 2 1
First edition

Contents

Introduction

A scant number of Gospel verses refer directly to Mary, the Mother of Jesus, but Christian reflection on her role and meaning in Christian belief and piety has filled volumes. One contemporary study center devoted to Mary boasts a library of over 100,000 pamphlets and books and an untold number of images. This written record gathers in a much larger unwritten tradition spanning the last twenty centuries and the majority of the globe. An ongoing popular tradition of devotion to Mary keeps renewing itself in an amazing variety of forms through the centuries. Young people give the Virgin of Guadalupe a prime place among their tattoos. A young man has no rosary beads but creates a rap rhythm to pray his story while tracking the traditional patterns of prayers.

This book has the modest goal of presenting a readable overview that clarifies the main points of Christian tradition about Mary by tracing the historical background leading up to the present day. We will also be tying tradition to contemporary concerns, because the Marian tradition is wondrously flexible. The words that Vatican II used to express the outlook of the "Church in the Modern World" toward the human family could truly be applied to the way that Christian believers have experienced Mary—"The joy and hope, the grief and anguish of the [people] of our time, especially of those who are poor or afflicted in any way are the joy and hope, the grief and anguish of the followers of Christ [and Mother of God] as well." These words express succinctly the way that Christians have experienced Mary and have responded to her.

Ways of thinking about Mary, known as Mariology, have often been talked about in terms of a "high" Mariology and a "low" Mariology. Each represents a helpful angle of vision on a multifaceted tradition. When we think about Mary in terms of what is unique about her—her special privileges and experiences—we are expressing a high Mariology. When we speak of Mary in terms of the characteristics that she shares with the rest of humanity, we are operating from a low Mariology. Neither approach has more truth or is more respectful than the other. In fact, we need both of them together to navigate a very complex subject without losing track of important realities. The Church has valued and honored both approaches. When the early Church argued about the best way to understand the nature of Christ, the humanity of his mother was integral to their conviction that he was fully human. Meditation on Mary's privileges has been a way to honor the courage she showed in agreeing to be the Mother of Jesus with all the unknown demands that might entail.

Much of what is written here is written from the point of view of Roman Catholic Christians. The foundational beliefs about Mary, however, were established before there was any division of Orthodox or Roman Catholic. This is also true about Christians who follow various movements that developed from the Reformation. That said, Orthodox and Roman Catholics have been more comfortable with high Mariology than the Reformation traditions have been. This is especially true of the doctrines of the Immaculate Conception and Assumption that have a long history of tradition but are less directly tied to Scripture.

We will begin each chapter by gathering up some mental equipment for the path ahead. These are background ideas that will help to illuminate the material in that chapter. Each chapter ends with reflection questions and suggestions for further reading.

CHAPTER 1
Mary in the Scriptures

The actual biblical texts referring to Mary are few in number but rich in content. They have played a powerful and varied role in the life of the Christian church, particularly in the Orthodox and Roman Catholic churches. Over the centuries of meditation on Mary, Christians have turned to these texts for many purposes—to mine them for poetic images and honorific titles, to call on them as supports for doctrinal pronouncements (especially about the nature of Jesus), to ground expectations of ideal female virtue, to voice public prayer, to sustain private devotion, and to provide companionship in the endurance of deep suffering to name but a few.

In this chapter, we will look at contemporary interpretations of scriptural references to Mary. We will also explore briefly some of the early Christian texts that were not accepted into the official Scriptures, which form the basis for a number of familiar popular stories that "fill in the blanks" of the biblical account. Before taking up the texts themselves, we first need to consider some of the ways that contemporary biblical scholars approach the interpretation of texts.

TOOLS FOR INTERPRETING THE TEXTS

When we look to the biblical witness for an understanding of Mary, we are participating in a much larger project because we take our place among those who need to know how a written text conveys its message. Four insights to understanding biblical texts help us grasp the biblical witness to Mary.

Historical-critical Method

This first approach is generally traced to the eighteenth century. At that time, scholars began to think of the biblical text as a historically situated text that could be explored using studies similar to those for other ancient texts. Here are just a few of the guiding questions we can apply as we consider what Scripture tells us about Mary:

- How was this text developed; what was the history of its production and editing?

- What kinds of literary forms (poetry, genealogy, story, history) are employed, and what do we know about how these forms of writing convey their message?
- Are the written forms preceded by a stage in which the community passed along its convictions, laws, poems, stories, or history orally?
- What were neighboring peoples thinking at this time in history?
- How do the ideas of neighboring peoples compare with the biblical world view?

Despite the fact that some scholars used these methods to deny any religious importance to the Scriptures, many faith communities, including Roman Catholicism, view this approach as acceptable and fruitful. (See *Dei Verbum*, 12.)

Cultural Anthropology

In the last third of the twentieth century, scholars have begun to pay more attention to the ways of thinking, valuing, and ordering life found among the peoples that produced the biblical texts. Such ways of thinking, valuing, and ordering life make up what we can call the culture—the way of life—of a people. When groups of people do not share the same culture, there is naturally some amount of disconnect in the ways they interpret and understand life. Such is the situation that creates a distance between contemporary people of a particular culture and the biblical peoples who gave birth to the Scriptures. This distance requires careful attention if we are to come to any accurate sense of what the biblical authors were trying to communicate. Cultural anthropology is the branch of study that addresses these issues, and the insights of these scholars have helped us become more aware of the worldview of the biblical traditions and how careful we must be about the assumptions we make when we slip into imagining that their understandings of life are identical to ours. Attention to the culture in which Mary lived her life can greatly enrich our understanding of her experience and meaning.

Reader Response

Still more recently (1970s), those who study written texts have begun to attend more closely to what the reader brings to his/her interpretation of a text. Similarly, biblical scholars have noted that readers understand the characters in Scripture stories through the information given in the text and their own experience of the world. The combination of the biblical text and lived experience form a complex, composite character that goes beyond the text and has diverse meanings in different cultural contexts.

The question that scholars have raised is whether the author embeds a meaning in the text, a meaning that remains there—timelessly available. An alternative view of written texts theorizes that the meaning is more like a meeting of the author's efforts and the understandings and expectations brought by the reader to the text.

As we will see, this habit of merging the world of the text and the reader's lived experiences in the world often operate unconsciously to shape believers' views of Mary and her significance. One significant contemporary set of issues about readers' presuppositions, for example, is presented by those who bring feminist questions to an interpretation of Scripture and particularly of Mary.

Feminist Questions , i·y , liberation

It is important to begin by saying that "feminist" as it is intended here cannot be dismissed as a man-hating or anti-family stance. Simply stated, a feminist perspective desires the same respect, safety, and dignity for one's daughters and sisters as for one's sons and brothers. Christians today, both women and men, encourage the creation of this kind of world by being alert to attitudes or assumptions that make life narrow, dangerous, or demeaning for any individual or group of people. Some questions that could profitably be brought to the Scripture texts about Mary might be: How might attitudes toward women in any particular historical period or society color our understanding of Mary? Are there attitudes toward Mary that might create unhealthy or unrealistic ideals for women? Do the models of female virtue generated from the Mary of the Scriptures promote the dignity and wholeness of women? What does Mary offer to the human flourishing of women?

THE GOSPEL TEXTS

The Gospel texts about Mary can be grouped into those embedded in the infancy narratives of Matthew and Luke and the few others in which she appears in Jesus' public life. These latter are often spoken of as evidence of her discipleship.

The Infancy Narratives

The Gospels of Matthew and Luke each contain an infancy narrative, an account of how Jesus' entrance into human history was announced and took place. It is important that we orient ourselves from the beginning to the fact that these accounts are fundamentally about Jesus. As the Gospel writers made the case for Jesus' significance as the Messiah, Mary figured in *that* story as a key player. Luke's account gives the most prominent place to Mary, and that is where we will begin.

In his version of the infancy narrative, Luke lays out a pattern that would have been familiar to the first Christians who were steeped in the Hebrew Scriptures. This pattern emphasized the Hebrew belief that each child was conceived by the will of God. For those children who came to be extraordinary leaders, we find scriptural accounts of their conception that draw our attention to the action of their conception. This intervention was signaled by including certain details in the account: evidence of long-standing childlessness, an announcement by an angel, doubt and fear on the part of the person receiving the message, and a sign given by the messenger. For example, Raymond Brown, noted biblical scholar and theologian, points to the stories of the well-established barrenness of these women. Such stories make it clear that each woman *only* becomes pregnant through the power of God: Isaac's mother Sarah (see Genesis 18:11), Samson's mother (see Judges 13:2), and Hannah, the mother of the prophet Samuel (see 1 Samuel 1:19).

In Luke, we see the "special conception" form used not once, but twice. Before Mary even appears, Luke describes the conception of John the Baptist (Luke 1:5–24). The account includes the information that Elizabeth was barren and "getting on in years." There is a messenger from God who speaks to her husband, Zechariah. We see fear and doubt on Zechariah's part and the giving of a sign. For those familiar with the pattern from the Hebrew Scriptures, it is clear that the child to be born to this elderly couple will be someone special whose unique role is willed by God. This is like hearing a familiar musical fanfare. In the announcement of Jesus' conception, the theme is repeated at double volume.

The Annunciation

The angel's announcement to Mary follows the pattern of the annunciation of a special birth. "Behold, you will conceive in your womb and bear a son, and you shall name him Jesus. He will be great and will be called Son of the Most High, and the Lord God will give him the throne of David his father, and he will rule over the house of Jacob forever, and of his kingdom there will be no end" (Luke 1:31–33). Mary's question at this point highlights the fact that this child is exceptional by another degree. "How can this be, since I have no relations with a man?" Mary will conceive not after the failure of human efforts, she will conceive in the absence of any human act at all. In this case, God's will and power are more sharply emphasized as is the greater distinctiveness of her child. Thus Jesus' conception, through intervention by God, parallels that of certain Old Testament figures and of John the Baptist. At the same time, Jesus is clearly set off to a unique degree.

At this point Mary is satisfied with the explanation by the angel and says, "Behold, I am the handmaid of the Lord. May it be done to me according to your word" (Luke 1:38). Much has been written about this scene as a manifestation of Mary's virtue of obedience. It is just as valid to call her reply "assent," a less passive and more dynamic term that gives more weight to her reply as a free choice. It also upholds a vision of virtue for women that is less childlike, more responsible, and likely to encourage thoughtful responsibility for oneself. For while it is true that Mary is upheld as an example of virtue for all Christians, her virtues have often been more strongly recommended to women.

As we will see, Matthew's Gospel focuses on Joseph's side of the story but also describes the conception of Jesus as having taken place before Mary and Joseph came to live together. Scholars note that Matthew and Luke tell the story of Jesus' conception and birth very differently but retain this detail of an unusual conception. For this reason, it seems that both evangelists must have been drawing from more widespread stories retained in Christian tradition.

It is important to be clear here that there is no support in these Gospel accounts for the view that Jesus' conception by the intervention of the Holy Spirit rather than through human sexual activity is a message about sexuality being somehow linked to sin. It is equally inaccurate to imagine that Luke portrays the absence of sexual activity as a claim of Mary's sinlessness or purity. First-century Israelites drew from Genesis the conviction that God created humanity male and female, pronounced this creation "good," and told them to cleave to one another and to be fruitful. Furthermore, the injunction to be fruitful took on increased significance in the light of the covenant by which God promised to make Abraham the father of many descendants. (See Exodus 17.) Sexual activity resulting in the conception of children was a valued participation in both the work of creation and the covenant promise.

At this point we can refer back to reader response theory and remind ourselves that the simple text of the annunciation does not say what Mary was doing at this moment. Even so, numerous masterpieces of art depicting the annunciation by the angel have populated the Christian imagination with Mary in various attitudes, costumes, hairstyles, and physiques—depending on the imaginative ideals of the artist and his or her culture. As imaginative creations, none of these needs to be considered historically sacrosanct; there is even room for our own costuming, imagination, questions, and possibilities.

By Comparison

The conception of Jesus as portrayed in Matthew's Gospel puts us in touch with the culture of Mary's time and reminds us to anchor our imaginations in her reality. The unusual conception of Mary's child had a concrete consequence for Mary. Matthew says that Joseph became aware that Mary was pregnant during their betrothal (already a state of marital commitment), but before they had come to live together. The Gospel says that Joseph, "since he was a righteous man, yet unwilling to expose her to shame, decided to divorce her quietly" (Matthew 1:19–20). Deuteronomy prescribes that a woman found at her marriage not to be a virgin should be stoned. (See Deuteronomy 20–27.) It seems, though, that this prescription was not uniformly carried out in first-century Galilee. Nonetheless, a woman with a child and no husband would have been condemned to disgrace and to a future of dire insecurity. Salvation from this fate is one of the consequences of the angel's assurance to Joseph that the child is conceived by the Holy Spirit and that the marriage should go forward. Shortly thereafter, we read that Joseph names Mary's child Jesus. By this act of naming, he formally claims the child as his own, a legitimate child in the line of David.

After the account of the angel's words of reassurance to

Joseph, Matthew adds, "All this took place to fulfill what had been spoken by the Lord though the prophet: 'Behold, the virgin shall be with child and bear a son, and they shall name him Emmanuel,...'" (Matthew 1:23). Here Matthew is quoting Isaiah 7:14 and using the quote for his own purposes—to show how Jesus is the fulfillment of God's plan as set forth by the prophets. Matthew is following the Septuagint version of the Hebrew Scriptures, a Greek translation produced by Jewish scholars around the second century before Christ. The Septuagint used the Greek word for "virgin" to translate this text. The Hebrew original meant "young maiden." Most biblical commentators agree that the Jewish understanding of Isaiah was not that a literal virgin would conceive. Later, Christian reflection on the passage brought an important emphasis to the term "virgin."

In Matthew's Gospel, Mary never speaks, and the all-important encounter with the angel involves only Joseph. The story of Joseph's dilemma is prefaced by the genealogy of Jesus, traced from father to son for what Matthew counts as a total of forty-two generations. Embedded in this account of fathers and sons are four women. Tamar poses as a prostitute to obtain progeny from her dead husband's father. Rehab is a Canaanite prostitute who hides the Israelites who have come to spy in her land. Ruth is the foreign widow of an Israelite who has to take matters into her own hands to claim a husband from among her husband's relatives. The wife of Uriah is taken from her husband by King David who subsequently has her husband murdered. She becomes the

women in precarious situations

mother of Solomon and bargains to ensure that he will inherit David's throne.

The evidence of these women in the family tree of Jesus shows us that Mary's precarious situation was not unprecedented in Jesus' lineage. Their difficult situations and their daring responses were written into the history of salvation. Mary, though she does not speak, is clearly in this lineage.

The Visitation and Magnificat

In Luke's Gospel, the Annunciation to Mary is followed immediately by her visit to her elderly, pregnant relative, Elizabeth. (See Luke 1:39–56.) Elizabeth's lovely greeting to her ("Most blessed are you among women, and blessed is the fruit of your womb") has been take up as part of the ancient and beloved prayer addressed to Mary. Elizabeth's greeting, combined with that of the angel to Mary, begins the Hail Mary. We can find spiritual writers recommending this prayer by the end of the first thousand years of the Christian era.

Elizabeth addresses Mary as "the mother of my Lord," a phrase that puts her in line with Luke's final understanding of Jesus' identity. This phrase will also be called upon in the early centuries of the church as preachers and teachers try to formulate precisely what can accurately be said of Jesus. Is he human? Is he divine to the "same degree" as the God who creates? The Gospel story of Mary will become an anchor for both Jesus' humanity and his unity as a single person, as we will see when we consider Marian dogmas in Chapter 2.

Elizabeth ends her greeting with the statement, "Blessed are you who believed that what was spoken to you by the Lord would be fulfilled." Luke has laid out his Gospel to highlight this faith of Mary's. Both Mary and Zechariah had received a visit from an angel, but Mary had responded with the greater confidence in God's plans. The angel chides Zechariah "because you did not believe my words, which will be fulfilled at their proper time" (1:20). Luke will return to this example of Mary's faithfulness when he places her in the Upper Room with the Apostles and disciples after Jesus' ascension. The song of Mary, the Magnificat, is her response to Elizabeth as well as to her entire experience to this point. Here she speaks not only as a single individual but with the voice of the early Jewish-Christian community. Jeremiah and Isaiah, as well as the Psalms and voices from the Torah, echo throughout her song. Her psalm of praise for God's mercy to the lowly and fidelity to the covenant promises is entirely consistent with the prophets of the Hebrew Scriptures who also voiced these themes. Furthermore, they are themes that Luke takes up for special emphasis in his Gospel. It is particularly informative to notice the underlying voice of the prophets, because their cry represents God's rejection of the oppressive use of power against the lowly and defenseless. As much as this is a song about spiritual riches, it is also an examination of conscience about the concrete situation of the defenseless of our own times. To pray the Magnificat is to align ourselves with God's desire that the lowly be lifted up.

This hymn is also a foreshadowing of Jesus' own mission as he expressed in the Nazareth synagogue:

> The Spirit of the Lord is upon me
> because he has anointed me
> to bring glad tidings to the poor.
> He has sent me to proclaim liberty to captives
> and recovery of sight to the blind,
> to let the oppressed go free,
> and to proclaim a year acceptable to the Lord.
>
> LUKE 4:18–19, QUOTING ISAIAH 61

A phrase from the Catholic baptismal rite for infants names a child's parents his or her "first teachers in the faith." In this light, one might attribute Jesus' original religious understandings of his Jewish belief and practice to Mary and Joseph.

The Birth of Jesus

Luke uses the device of the census to bring Mary and Joseph to Bethlehem (a location that agrees with the tradition expressed in Matthew) for Jesus' birth. As Mary lays him in a makeshift bed and receives the visitation of the shepherds, we continue to hear echoes of Luke's message—Jesus comes to and for the lowly. Already in the Gospel Jesus has been called "Lord," "Son of the Most High," and one who will sit on "the throne of David, his father, forever." The shepherds now receive the news that he is also Savior and Messiah. After their visitation, "Mary kept all these things reflecting on them in her heart" (Luke 2:19).

Jesus is described in the text as Mary's "firstborn son." This is not a statement about whether she did or did not have other sons. Here it simply marks him as the child who will have the obligations and privileges the Law gave to a firstborn son. (See, for example, Numbers 3:12–13; 18:15–16; Deuteronomy 21:15–17.) The text also gives us no clue about the manner of Jesus' birth. We will take up that question in Chapter 2 along with other considerations of Catholic dogmas.

Reinforcing Mary, Joseph, and Jesus as faithful Israelites is the brief statement that Jesus was circumcised on the eighth day and named as the angel had designated. After this, the infancy narrative moves to the Temple, where it will conclude all that we know of Mary's life during Jesus' childhood.

Incidents in the Temple

Just as Luke began his Gospel with the appearance of an angel in the Temple announcing John's birth to Zechariah, Luke ends his infancy account in the Temple with two incidents: the presentation, which includes the encounters with Simeon and Anna; and the losing and finding of the boy Jesus. Each of these gives particular attention to Mary. The first of these, the presentation, once again portrays Jesus and his parents as faithful Jews fulfilling the requirements of the Law. In the process, they come upon two witnesses of Israel's desire for redemption. The first of these, the aged Simeon, gives voice to two of Luke's convictions about the Messiah. As Isaiah had said generations earlier, God's salvation will fulfill God's covenant promises while offering salvation to the Gentiles as well. (See Isaiah 42:6; 46:13; 49:6.)

Simeon goes on to address Mary, "Behold, this child is destined for the fall and rise of many in Israel, and to be a sign that will be contradicted (and you yourself a sword will pierce) so that the thoughts of many hearts may be revealed" (Luke 2:34–35). In time, Jesus' mission challenges people's deepest loyalties, and the conflict Simeon raises will not bypass Mary but run right through her. Was it any comfort to Mary when the prophetess, Anna, spoke her gratitude and hopes about the redeeming nature of the appearance of this child?

The final Temple encounter is the familiar story that takes place when Jesus is twelve and he remains in Jerusalem while his family started back home after the Passover pilgrimage. After three anxious days, they find him in the Temple, "sitting in the midst of the teachers, listening to them and asking them questions, and all who heard him were astounded at his understanding and his answers." Mary says what any parent would say, "Son why have you done this to us?" Jesus' explanation is that they should have known that he had to be "in my Father's house." Luke simply states (not surprisingly) that "they did not understand what he said to them." And once more, "his mother kept all these things in her heart" (Luke 2:41–51).

Luke's description of Mary during Jesus' conception, birth and childhood is a series of glorious promises and anxious realities—something, perhaps, not that distant from parenthood itself. Mary clearly is one who believes the word of God, but her believing is not blind. She faces much that must be pondered, including, according to Simeon, the life and death divisions over who Jesus is and what he demands. It is in the synoptic Gospels (Matthew, Mark, and Luke) that Mary's discipleship faces these questions.

Discipleship: Synoptic Gospels and Acts of the Apostles

The Gospel writers vary greatly in their descriptions of Mary's discipleship—the extent to which she committed herself to Jesus' mission and message during his lifetime. Mark, the earliest of the Gospels, includes Mary in a devastating account of Jesus' family trying to rein him in and bring an end to his teaching mission. As we have seen, Luke's Acts of the Apostles places her among the Apostles and other loyal followers gathered in the Upper Room after Jesus' ascension. What are we to make of this range of readings?

The first thing we might understand is that Mary's role in Jesus' adult life had more to do with the familiar stresses of motherhood than with her serene statues and paintings. Our understanding of Mary's concrete, conflicted human situation has been greatly enhanced by recent use of anthropological and historical information by Scripture scholars. This helps us flesh out our understanding of the life she lived. It also helps us to connect it to real life today. Mary, as she is portrayed in Mark, is clearly understandable in light of the first century Palestinian situation.

Nazareth of the first century has been described by biblical scholars as a village of poor farmers and artisans—all living a hand-to-mouth existence without economic security or cushion. They lived as people of an occupied land who were taxed into desperation by Temple, King Herod, and Rome. They lived in constant threat from uprisings and the occupying army's brutal response. In 4 BC, for example, two thousand Jewish men were crucified in the suppression of a rebellion. Needless to say, this setting was a time and place where it would be extremely dangerous to go about proclaiming the arrival and final triumph of the kingdom of God.

Knowing this social history helps us realize the plain practical wisdom of Jesus' mother and other family members in their initial reaction to his mission of proclaiming God's kingdom. The earliest of these accounts appears in Mark (Mark 3:20–21, 31–35). As a crowd gathers around Jesus so large that he and the disciples could not even eat, his family "went out to restrain him, for people were saying 'He has gone out of his mind.'" Given the volatile and repressive political situation, it makes perfect sense that those who cared most about him would try to protect him from the real and dire consequences of his behavior. When Jesus is told that "his mother and brothers" are asking for him, he says, "Who are my mother and my brothers?" And looking at those who sat around him, he said, "Here are my mother and my brothers! Whoever does the will of God is my brother and sister and mothers." This response performs a shocking replacement of the "natural" family with a new set of relationships—the community of those committed to God's will as expressed in Jesus' teaching. The later Gospels omit the embarrassing aspects of the family's mission. They also soften (Matthew 12:46–50) or omit (Luke 8:19–20) any radical contrast Jesus makes between his natural family and the new community of his disciples.

Discipleship: Gospel of John

In John's Gospel, Mary is actually never named—but only described—as Jesus' mother. She appears in two very brief but poignant scenes that stand as bookends at the beginning and end of his ministry. In her first appearance, she is at a marriage feast in Cana (John 2:1–11) where she seems to understand the bridal couple better than she does her son. She simply points out to Jesus that they have no wine, certainly an extremely embarrassing situation. Jesus reprimands her for her poor timing, "Woman, how does your concern affect me? My hour has not yet come." Nonetheless, Jesus does change water into wine in an act that constitutes his first "sign," a manifestation of God's power acting in him. Mary is described afterward as traveling with Jesus and his disciples, so it is clear that John saw her as a believer and disciple from the beginning.

The only other place she appears in this Gospel is at the foot of the cross. "When Jesus saw his mother and the disciple there whom he loved, he said to his mother, 'Woman, behold, your son.' Then he said to the disciple, 'Behold, your mother.' And from that hour the disciple took her into his home" (John 19:26–27). Here she is not only faithful in her presence, but it is assumed that she will remain with Jesus' most intimate followers after his death.

Book of Revelation

In addition to the mentions of Mary in the Gospels and the Acts of the Apostles, there is a passage of the book of Revelation that Christians gradually came to apply to Mary. Revelation belongs to a type of literature called apocalyptic. This is a highly symbolic and dramatic form of writing that is meant to encourage oppressed people to have hope. This form of writing uses symbols so that the writer can criticize the powers-that-be without fear of retaliation. The message of hope assures the sufferers that God will bring the oppressors to the punishment they deserve and will reward the faithful. The time at which justice will prevail is often portrayed as the end of the world or the end of the present age. In the New Testament, the book called *Revelation* or *The Apocalypse* seems to have been a message to the suffering churches of the Roman empire. These Christians were persecuted for refusing to worship the Roman gods or emperors who were considered divine.

Among the many figures in the book are fearsome beasts, monsters, and evil persons representing the Roman empire, a sacrificial lamb and a newborn child representing

Jesus, and angels who carry out God's rescue of the faithful. In Chapter 12, "a great sign appeared in the sky, a woman clothed with the sun, with the moon under her feet, and on her head a crown of twelve stars." She gives birth to a child who is threatened by a "huge red dragon," but her son "was caught up to God and his throne. The woman herself fled into the desert where she had a place prepared by God…" (Revelation 12:1–6). At the time of its writing, this passage was probably meant to represent God's protection of the persecuted Church. The woman's cosmic attributes can be traced back to the Genesis story of Joseph's dream in which the stars represented the tribes of Israel, the people of God of whom Jesus is born. (See Genesis 37:9.)

The writings of early Christian teachers first apply this passage to Mary in the fifth century. Catholics are very accustomed to assuming that it originally applied to Mary because of the tradition of reading it at Mass on Marian feasts and from well-known paintings of Mary that show her with the moon under her feet and a crown of twelve stars.

Bonus: Non-canonical Texts

"Wait!" you might say. "What about Mary's parents, Anne (or Anna) and Joachim? You haven't talked about them. Where do they come in the Scripture story? And what about her childhood?" You may have heard stories of Mary's parents and childhood right along with the stories from Scripture, and probably no distinction was ever made. Religious art includes portraits of Mary's parents, of a childhood spent in the Temple, of her betrothal to Joseph with his character-istic staff topped by a lily, and of Mary reading a book at the moment when the angel Gabriel appeared to her. The fact is, however, that nothing of Mary's life before her encounter with the angel is told in the Gospels or anywhere else in the Scriptures.

So where do these details come from? They are described in a number of texts produced from the second through thirteenth centuries. These were never accepted into the of-ficial list of books that makes up the New Testament. Such an authoritative list of books is called the canon, so these books are sometimes called non-canonical. The Christian churches have not given them the status of divine revelation. One might think of them in the way we regard television movies or novels "based on" a historical event or person. In other words, details were added in an imaginative way to "fill in the blanks" of an accepted account.

These early writings include the *Gospel of Thomas*, the *Gospel of Mary* (Magdalene), and the *Protevangelium of James*. Various judgments kept them out of the New Testa-ment, particularly questions about their late age of com-position—and thus their inability to count as witnesses from the age of the Apostles. They were also judged to be beyond the scope of the Christian consensus about what could properly be taught about Jesus. The *Protevangelium of James* and the other texts, like the *Gospel of Pseudo-Matthew* and the *Gospel of the Birth of Mary*, popularized its teachings while providing answers to questions that the

New Testament did not touch. Although most of us have not read these texts, they would seem very familiar, because many artists have incorporated them into their portrayals of Mary's life. We may also have heard preaching that did not differentiate between the information in the Gospels and other early Christian writings. In fact, early Christian teachers and preachers did not always distinguish between such books and the information they obtained from the Gospels.

Non-canonical writing has contributed many non-Gospel details to Mary's life. They name Mary's parents, tell of her going to live in the Temple at the age of three, and say that she made a perpetual vow of virginity, which is portrayed as a preparation for her becoming the mother of Jesus. Her future role is told to her by an angel, and her whole life is a preparation for what is to come. Her marriage to an aged Joseph is, in some texts, clearly not consummated, and she is accompanied both in the Temple and in her married life by a group of dedicated virgins in a life that seems to be modeled on a monastic ideal. In one source, she is also declared a perpetual virgin by a midwife who attends Jesus' birth. The end of her life is never mentioned in Scripture, but a number of the apocryphal texts describe her death in detail and depict Jesus raising Mary's body to heaven before it has a chance to decay in the tomb.

The various written versions of these stories were widespread and even translated into different languages. They helped people satisfy their curiosity about Mary and Jesus beyond the very limited information given in the Gospels. They were also useful for subgroups who wanted to encourage particular teachings about the meaning of Christian belief. Although they were never adopted as approved Scriptures, these writings were often assumed to be historical; sometimes they were even written in the name of one of the Apostles or other respected historical figure. Material from them definitely entered the Christian imagination, is widely found in Christian art, and found its way into preaching and writing, often without being distinguished from the Gospels.

CONCLUSION

This brief survey outlines for us the sources of our understanding of Mary and sorts out the scriptural from the non-scriptural record. From these few references, Catholic Christians have constructed an impressive edifice of devotion and doctrine. In the chapters to follow, we will describe this heritage and hold it in the light of today to see what might be particularly enriching for us and to ask how Christians of today might be enriching the ever-living tradition.

REFLECTION QUESTIONS

1. *What images do you bring to the annunciation text? What is Mary doing? How is she dressed? What is her attitude? What happens if you read the text while imagining her dressed and occupied as a young woman of your own time and place?*

2. *What kind of preaching and spiritual interpretation have you heard about Mary's conceiving Jesus while still a virgin? Has this preaching affected your views of your own sexuality? If so, in what ways?*

3. *What verses of the Magnificat speak most strongly to you? In what ways are you powerful and in what ways are you lowly? How can the Gospel be said to be "good news" for the powerful? How do you react to the idea that there are politically/economically relevant verses in this poem?*

4. *How do you react to the notion that Mary had to learn gradually to embrace Jesus' mission and message? What does that say to you about your own discipleship?*

5. *Do you see Mary as someone chiefly like us in her human experience, or do you see her chiefly as someone awesome and unique? Have your interpretations of her varied over time and circumstances, or have they been more fixed?*

6. *Find a copy of the nativity story as illustrated by Julie Vivas (*The Nativity, *Voyager Books, 2006). How do you react to her illustrations of Mary, Joseph, and Jesus?*

FOR FURTHER READING

Mary in the New Testament. Raymond E. Brown, Karl P. Donfried, Joseph A. Fitzmyer, and John Reumann, eds. Philadelphia: Fortress Press, 1978.

Mary According to Women. Carol Frances Jegen, ed. Kansas City: Sheed and Ward, 1985.

Johnson, Elizabeth A. *Dangerous Memories: A Mosaic of Mary in Scripture*. New York: Continuum, 2004.

———. *Truly Our Sister: A Theology of Mary in the Communion of Saints*. New York: Continuum, 2003.

CHAPTER 2
Mary in Church Teaching

I once introduced myself to a woman at church who was accompanied by a small daughter. When I ask the woman her daughter's name she simply said, "Her name is Margaret, but we should have named her "Treasure." I remember that brief meeting as a vivid reminder of the reality that some experiences are too large for a conventional container. No ordinary name could convey this mother's experience of the gift of her child. Have you ever had an experience that was too amazing or too awful to be put into words? Have you struggled to communicate that to someone else or even to explain it to yourself? Have you ever been taken aback by a child's drawing or the kind of brilliant, logic-defying explanations they use to convey their understanding of life's mysteries: death or separation, love or pain? Remembering such experiences is going to be very helpful as we delve into the mysteries of Christian teaching about Mary.

What I mean by this is that the faith experience that the Church tries to put into an explicit teaching will always be larger than its finite container of concepts and words. This is because Christian teaching arises out of the experience of being a disciple of Jesus Christ. It tries to convey the amazing fact of the free gift of intimate relationship between God and humanity. It is an attempt to spell out the implications of that gift and their consequences for life. Any attempt to put this wonder into words will be limited by the fact of trying to contain the infinite in a finite formula. Any specific teaching on any topic depends on an overarching belief that God chooses to be in loving relationship with humanity and has made that choice most concrete in an actual historical person, Jesus of Nazareth. In our present culture, the deductions of science are the privileged kind of container for knowledge. Religious language at times can be closer to poetry. Both ways of thinking and speaking try to convey truth using very different tools.

In this chapter, we will be looking at the teaching of the Christian churches on Mary, the Mother of this Jesus. We will include the most foundational official teachings of the Roman Catholic Church: Mary can be called the Mother of God; she was conceived without original sin; at the end of her life, her body was assumed into heaven; and she is fittingly called "the *Virgin* Mary." We will also look at the title "co-redemptrix" that is currently a matter of much discussion among some Catholics.

EQUIPMENT TO AID IN READING THIS CHAPTER

To outfit ourselves for the discussion in this chapter, we will need 1) an understanding of what the Church means by dogma; 2) some perspective on our experiences of confusion or doubt in regard to Church teaching; 3) a basic understanding of what we mean by Eastern and Western Christianity; 4) a historical perspective on Marian teachings; and 5) a firm grounding in the centrality of Jesus Christ in everything said about Mary.

Dogma, Doctrine, and Theological Opinion

The most important teachings of the Church have come to be called dogmas. Christians believe that God chooses to communicate with humanity. They call this communication revelation. Revelation is not, first of all, a list of beliefs or moral mandates; rather, it is the offer of loving relationship. This is conveyed through our experience of ongoing creation and human living, through the history of the Hebrew people as described in the Scriptures; in the life, death, and resurrection of Jesus who is believed to be the Christ; and in the enduring companionship of the Holy Spirit among us in the Church.

The Church understands itself as having a unique responsibility for passing on that revelation, and so understands itself as uniquely gifted in the interpretation of revelation. Specific teachings do not replace the underlying message of unconditional love of God. They are meant to *serve* God's revelation—to make it more clear and available for successive generations. This is also the function of the belief that the Holy Spirit guides the Church and protects it from error in conveying the most central understandings of the relationship God offers. Not all formulations of belief are on equal footing, meaning that some are central and others play more of a supporting role.*

Some Christian teachings are considered revealed by God and essential to Christian identity. These central ideas, when defined by the Church, are called *dogmas*. These are found in the decisions of the councils of the early Church such as the declaration that Jesus is both fully human and fully divine. They are found in the ancient Christian creeds that are recited by Christians today in the sacrament of baptism and at the celebration of the Sunday Eucharist. Elements of the creed that Christians today take for granted are formulas resulting from struggle, generally after someone in the early Church had begun teaching something that felt "off" to a significant segment of the larger Church community. A process, sometimes taking decades or even centuries, would begin as rival viewpoints and were argued

---

*See, for example, the statement in the Vatican II document on ecumenism, *Unitatis Redintegratio*, in *Vatican Council II*, edited by Austin Flannery, OP. New York: Costello Publishing Company, 1975.

through. Those that have come down to us as orthodox teaching were argued out and agreed upon in those meetings of the world's bishops that are called ecumenical (or worldwide) councils.

Church here is meant to be the people of God, the baptized community. Church teachers do not invent teaching for the Church, but distill and express the Church's existing faith. Some beliefs, as we shall see, circulated in the Church for centuries before it was considered necessary to secure them in a dogmatic formula. At other times, a declaration of a dogma was meant as a celebration of God's grace, rather than as a defense of a threatened truth. We will see an example of this in the 1950 declaration of Mary's assumption.

Doctrines play a supporting role. They depend on or spell out the implications of dogma. Any expression of teaching is limited by the fact that revelation is always more than can ever be expressed in words. It will always be necessary to spell out dogma and doctrine in *theological opinions*. These formulations are not official definition, but are attempts to explain dogmas and doctrines for a given time and place. Faced with these formulations, we may find ourselves expressing doubts or disagreement.

Experiences of Confusion or Doubt

- Some people experience the Catholic dogmas about Mary: Mother of God, her virginity, immaculate conception, assumption—as rather self-evident. These are honors that God would, of course, bestow on Mary. We can simply and rightly appreciate and hold them in awe—even if many of us have only the vaguest notion of how they might be explained.

- Other people think that these are some of the strangest ideas they have ever met. How does one explain the assumption or the virgin birth? They defy common sense and normal human experience.

- Sometimes people are offended by them. Wasn't Mary human? Wouldn't she have the common human experiences of struggling with sin, laboring to give birth? And if she didn't, what good is she to us poor struggling creatures? And don't these "privileges" almost seem to denigrate ordinary human lives with their sexuality and other bodily concerns? It is almost cruel to hold her up as a humanly impossible model.

- For others, these matters seem irrelevant. Whether they can be adequately explained or not is of little concern. What could they possibly have to do with the ordinary Christian's efforts to be faithful to the Gospel in a complex world?

We can look at two perspectives that may help us approach these teachings constructively. The first realizes the difficulty of truly rejecting a Church dogma. This is an idea put forth by the great German theologian, Karl Rahner. Rahner is notable for his amazing body of theological writing, his complexity of thought and expression, and his deep, creative exploration of Church teaching. In addition to these scholarly concerns, he also had an abiding interest in the faith of ordinary people. During his long academic career, he regularly counseled penitents in confession and spoke at spirituality and education days for lay people. When commenting on Catholic dogma, Rahner noted that, in his view, it was very difficult for most of us fundamentally to repudiate a central Christian teaching. In order to do this, he argued, one would have to understand and reject the teaching in its full technical explanation, which very few people actually grasp. This means that for most people, questioning or exploring the complexities of our faith is not a source of spiritual danger. What a person is often rejecting is not what the heart of a dogma intends to teach, but some poorly expressed or understood explanation of that teaching.

A second perspective recognizes our inability to contain adequately divine matters in our limited concepts. Explanations of doctrines are more successful or less successful attempts to make the teaching understandable for believers. Some of the factors that will affect their success are the cultural, philosophical, material, language, and historical situation of the people developing or receiving the explanation. Much of what is argued about among different branches of Christianity or within each branch is the adequacy of theological explanations. This is also the source of much of the controversy that arises.

Doubt and controversy can be painful aspects of trying to understand and accept Church teaching. On the other hand, doubt is really recognition that the greatness of God is too much for our small containers. This acknowledgment is a way to honor the reality of God. For this reason, doubt can be an expression of faith. It acknowledges that no formulation of words *is* God.

Eastern and Western Christianity

From time to time, you will read about some theological idea or liturgical or devotional practice beginning in the "East" or becoming accepted in the "West." These are shorthand ways of describing two different styles of thinking, piety, and governance that have characterized Christianity from very early in its history. The East developed from Greek culture and included Greece, Asia Minor, and areas of the east coast of the Mediterranean. Constantine eventually established Constantinople as its capital. The West developed out of Roman Latin ways of viewing the world and included everything west of Italy, with Rome as its center. The western sections of North Africa would also be included. For many centuries, the two approaches considered themselves a single Christianity. Unfortunately, in 1054, an accumulation of theological, cultural, and political tensions produced a definitive break in this unity that lasts until today. In their present form, these churches are known as the Orthodox Catholic Church (East) and the Roman Catholic Church (West). The most basic teachings about Mary developed before the split and while there were differences of liturgical forms, art, and devotions, there was basic agreement in essentials.

A Sense of Incarnational History

None of the Church's teachings about Mary were instantly evident to everyone, everywhere, at all times. They have developed through a process of meditation, witness, spiritual experience, argumentation, prayer, and politics. Rather than be scandalized by the messiness of this process, believers can recognize in this the defining Christian belief—the incarnation. This belief refers, first of all, to the fact that God became fully human in Jesus Christ. This primary meaning also opens up a secondary meaning for incarnation. This is the fact that God chooses to come to humanity through humanity. The process of human dealings with one another is the process by which God communicates and guides the unfolding of faith. This also means that as human beings continue to change in their understanding and use of language and symbols, new ways of explaining faith are likely to develop. Not that we will suddenly decide something that contradicts one of the basic tenets of the faith, but our understandings and explanations can develop. This is the second reason not to fear our questions, confusion, and probing of our faith. Such is the process by which God can continue to unfold faith for new generations. At its best, such a process, guided by God's Spirit, will be characterized by the Spirit's fruits: "love, joy, peace, patience, kindness, generosity, faithfulness, gentleness, self-control" (Galatians 5:22–23). Keeping our eyes on the incarnate Christ is an integral part of our equipment for understanding Marian teachings.

The Centrality of Jesus the Christ

The development of the earliest Marian dogmas begins always at the same point. Accurate teaching about Christ is being threatened, and the Christian understanding of Mary helps to throw light on Jesus' identity. We saw in our exploration of Scripture that when Luke described Mary's virginal conception of Jesus, he was affirming God's sovereign power to give life and God's choice to exercise that power in a heightened way in the case of Jesus. Luke had no abstract interest in Mary's virginity outside this scenario. In the present chapter, we will see that the definition of a dogma affirming Mary as *Theotokos*, the bearer of God, originated in a need to defend clearly an adequate Christian understanding of Jesus. Since most people do not meet the Marian dogmas in the context of their originating arguments but in catechesis, song, and worship, it can be easy to miss this essential point of reference. Marian dogmas are best understood as expressions of the Christian desire to understand and teach accurately and adequately about Christ.

When a new situation, expression of belief, or behavior causes questions about what is genuine Christianity, the process of clarifying starts. This process draws on the Scriptures, current understanding of tradition, and practice of the Church's members. As we will see, the piety of the Church in general—what feasts people celebrate, what hymns they sing, or prayers they perpetuate—can also be indications of the genuine tradition. The Church's teaching about Mary is the result of such a process, a process that first began as an argument about Jesus. Equipped, now, for our journey, let us take up the story of those teachings.

MARY IN EARLIEST TEACHINGS

In the earliest centuries of the Church, there were several widespread disagreements about fundamental issues of Christian belief. Because we have been shaped by centuries of interpretation about him, it is very difficult to put ourselves back into the struggles of those who knew him in the flesh. According to the Gospels, his friends and followers knew his mother and family; they ate with him, saw his fatigue and discouragement, and saw him die. Even scriptural affirmations that he was the son of God don't flesh out how that is to be understood. It also says that he "in every respect has been tested as we are, yet without sin" (Hebrews 4:15).

As the first Christians struggled to preach and understand their experience of the unique person, Jesus Christ, two basic difficulties raised their heads repeatedly. Depending on their cultural and philosophical backgrounds, some listeners were likely to accept Christ's humanity but deny that he could really be divine. Others might accept his divinity and find it unacceptable that he could be human. At times, organized groups formed who believed and preached from each of these positions. Some of the earliest Christian reflections on Mary were intimately involved in these arguments and a part of clarifying these misunderstandings.

Compared to later centuries, it might seem strange to us that relatively little emphasis was put on Mary in the earliest days of the Church.* What was said of her focused on the humanity she shares with the rest of us. At that time, there were many mother goddesses among the gods worshiped by the different peoples of the Mediterranean. An emphasis on Mary or on her privileges and uniqueness would have been likely to give people the impression that Christianity also had several gods, among them the Great Mother that many people were accustomed to worshiping. The earliest Christian mentions of Mary outside the New Testament also show why a "low" Mariology was important.

We find some of this very early teaching in the letters of Ignatius of Antioch, a bishop in what is now Syria, who was martyred in about 110. We know something about his concerns and his way of explaining the Gospel because we have a handful of letters that he wrote to churches around the Mediterranean—probably only a few years after the writing of Saint John's Gospel. Ignatius engaged in controversy with a group who held what we call *Docetism*. They emphasized that God is eternal and unchanging—completely separate from anything material. How, they asked, could such a being be said to *become*, at some historical time, a limited human being who suffered and died? It was simply unthinkable—Christ must have been essentially a *divine* being who

---

*For the information here on earliest teaching about Mary, we are indebted to Hilda Graef's fine scholarship on Marian doctrines: *Mary: A History of Doctrine and Devotion*. Westminster, MD: Christian Classics, 1985.

only *appeared* to have a human body and only appeared to die.

In a letter to the Ephesians, Ignatius replied to such arguments. He explained that we can know that Christ is truly human with an actual human body because he had been "carried in the womb" of Mary. Mary was human and gave actual, human birth to Jesus. Ignatius depends on the testimony of Mary's pregnancy and giving birth to argue for Christ's full humanity. Let us keep in mind that Mary was not some kind of passive incubator, but gave her consent to God's proposal that she conceive a Savior through the Holy Spirit. So her participation in giving birth to Christ was fully human rather than merely physical.

Even today, it is helpful to consider this very ancient argument in order to ground us in the fact that Mary, whatever her honors or perfections, is above all human. This affirmation is not a diminishment of honor, but a way of recognizing her essential role in the Incarnation. This role became particularly important as Christians reflected on the source of their salvation. Christ, they believed, saved by taking on our humanity. If this Incarnation was incomplete or partial, we would not be fully saved. The belief that Jesus Christ only seemed to have a body, that Mary was not in flesh his mother (the heresy of Docetism), continued to be an argument against Christian teaching for centuries.

This and other issues concerning the Church's teaching about Christ needed clarification, as well. Did Christ really suffer and die, and how can one say that about a glorious and powerful God? Was Christ *fully* divine or some kind of middle being, greater than other creatures but created and not fully divine? If he was both human and divine, how was his identity configured? Was one part of him dominant and the other subordinate? Was he perhaps a composite—a divine nature replacing the soul within his human body?

Such questions played out across the first five and a half centuries of church history. Some of these questions were very divisive, and at different times and places, bishops, teachers, congregations, priests, and the emperor or empress could be found on each side. Because the councils that dealt with these questions took place so early in church history, before the schism between Orthodox and Roman Catholicism and before the Protestant Reformation, their teachings are considered foundational to all forms of Christianity. Church teachers continued to call on the Church's understanding of Mary to play a part in clarifying belief about Christ.

MARY AS *THEOTOKOS*: THE FOUNDATIONAL MARIAN DOGMA

Theotokos, a specially coined Greek term meaning "God bearer," had been used for Mary as part of an ancient creed at Alexandria, Egypt, perhaps as early as the second century. This title affirmed her important role but avoided the title "Mother of God" for the reasons mentioned above. In 431, an ecumenical (worldwide) council of bishops met at the city of Ephesus in what is now Turkey. Here they applied this title to Mary as a definitive Church teaching.

At this point in history, the bishops were struggling with the question of whether the human and the divine natures of Christ were ultimately a unity. Nestorius, bishop of Constantinople, had begun to teach that if Christ was both human and divine, Mary as human could not be the mother of God but only the mother of the human Jesus. Nestorius' description made Christ sound as though he could be two separate entities, something the majority of the bishops found unacceptable. One of the ways they found to express their conviction was by explicitly affirming that one needed to take as faith that Mary was the God-bearer. Just as she bore the human nature of Christ, and Christ being a single entity, she must also be called the bearer of his divinity in its entrance into human history. Here we have a dogmatic pronouncement being made about Mary, but in the context of clarifying the nature of Christ. Later, the Latin-speaking western Church translated *Theotoko* as "Mother of God," the term familiar to Roman Catholics today.

MARY AS VIRGIN

Unlike Mary as mother, Christian teaching on Mary as virgin has not received a definitive declaration because of some threat to essential belief. This dogma developed more organically from the New Testament, from early creedal statements, the writings of the Fathers of the Church, and repetition in statements by a number of popes.

In Chapter 1, we looked at what the New Testament has

to say about Mary's virginity. What Matthew and Luke were writing about was the virginal *conception*, meaning that Jesus was conceived without the participation of a man. This foundational scriptural understanding with its emphasis on God's power to give life and on Jesus' unique identity is commonly held by most forms of Christianity. Where denominations tend to differ is on the question of Mary's perpetual virginity. In its strongest form, this teaching is understood to include her lifelong virginity before, during, and after Jesus' birth. The title *Ever-Virgin* is often understood to express this doctrine, which is the official doctrine of Roman Catholicism.

The virginity tradition is complex, because virginity can be defined as a physical state. This rather straightforward understanding is complicated, however, by the different ways people through the centuries have: 1) understood human biology, and 2) given a cultural meaning to virginity. At times this tradition has been misused to mark marriage, married sexuality, and parenthood as a second-class vocation. As Karl Rahner emphasizes in *Mary, Mother of the Lord*, these elements of Christian life can never be considered undesirable, since they are distinguished by their own sacrament. For this reason, he argues, it should not be assumed that Mary's holiness required that she be perpetually a virgin, as though she would have been less holy leading a usual married life.

While the Hebrew tradition did not give a privileged place to virginity, as Christianity spread beyond its Jewish origins, a different attitude gradually developed. The tradition of the virginal conception is found in two Gospels and, as we have seen, Christians have interpreted Isaiah 7:14—"a virgin (young maiden) shall conceive and bear a son"—as a reference to Jesus. The rather minimal references to Mary in Scripture were supplemented by apocryphal writings popularly attributed to Apostles or other early teachers but never taken up into the canon of Scripture. Some of these, especially the *Protevangelium of James,* have a great deal to say about Mary's virginity; not all preachers and teachers distinguished between such writings and what came to be recognized as the authoritative Gospels. The tradition is further described and developed by the Fathers of the Church. These are teachers and preachers, many of them bishops, who were active in the first six centuries of Christianity and whose existing writings give us a priceless window into the development of Christian doctrine and practice. Finally, the tradition is carried by the expressions of devotion and worship practiced by baptized believers.

Several traditional concerns behind this teaching have to do with Mary's role as the Mother of God, which was the focus of her uniqueness. As with other Marian doctrines, this is really an expression of how one should think about the person who was God's mother. What would be a suitable state for that person? There was an early assumption that such a person ought to be sinless in two ways: free from original sin and free from personal sin. This sense of Mary's purity extended itself into a belief that she was perpetually a virgin—a conviction that expresses a particular understanding of *purity*. In order to understand that perspective, we need to examine some historical attitudes toward sexuality and the body.

Studies of the early Roman Empire's culture have found that virginity was not a value in the Roman Empire, because Roman citizens had an obligation to marry and reproduce so that there would be a supply of new citizens for the empire. Life was dangerous, and life expectancy was short; the empire needed constant rebuilding of its pool of citizens. Early Christianity, however, gradually generated its own set of priorities. Asceticism, that is self-denial for religious motivation, developed into a highly valued lifestyle in the early Church.

Especially from the third century on, asceticism was often expressed as virginity. Other forms of sexual asceticism were also considered desirable—refraining from sexual activity in marriage or remaining unmarried after being widowed—but virginity was the most prized. The motivation and meaning of the practice differed widely with time and place though overlap and mixing were common. Three configurations offer a sampling. First, the early church, with varying degrees of intensity, understood itself to be in the last age of history, which was signaled by Jesus' resurrection. Life was assessed with this brevity in mind and, as Paul said, the goal was to adopt a lifestyle that would prepare one for the final day. (See 1 Corinthians 7:25–31.) A second motivation also looked toward the end of time. Some Christians chose to remain unmarried, to abstain from sexual relations in marriage, or to refrain from further marriage, even when widowed very young, as a way to resist the Roman duty to reproduce. Perhaps, as some historians have noted, the Christians expected that their resistance would shrink the population of citizens, hasten the fall of the Empire, and help bring about the final kingdom of God.

Third, in the cultural worldview that shaped the Roman empire, stoicism was an admired and widespread ideal. This system of philosophy valued serene, reasoned responses to all life's situations and considered the passions an obstacle to that life. Theirs was a very subtle and nuanced way of thinking. They did not broadly dismiss all emotion; rather, they prized self-control and the priority of reason. They believed that sexual intercourse and childbirth had the potential to disturb this control but could be reconciled with this world view because of their useful ends. Sexuality in marriage was to be measured and directed toward its reasonable end, procreation. At the same time, it could also contribute to the affectionate bond of the couple. In some settings, celibate Christians called attention to their admirable, or even superior, mode of life by outdoing the Stoics and refraining from all sexual activity. For these and other reasons, virginity began to be considered superior to marriage by many Christian teachers.

Contrary to the social practices of the surrounding culture, young women dedicated to virginity lived with their families or groups of virgins, and widows lived in common as an ascetic practice. The childhood of Mary, described in the *Protevangelium of James,* includes a vow of virginity at the age of three and a childhood in the Temple in the company of a group of young virgins. From our historical perspective, we know that nothing like this practice existed in the Israelite religion of Mary's time, but was considered at the time of its writing to be a reflection of the spiritually-ideal life for a girl destined to be the mother of Christ. Mary, in turn, became the model for a ultimately virtuous young woman.

The vow of the *Protevagelium* can help us differentiate between the concerns of the Gospel tradition and the concerns of later writers and teachers. The Gospels make no direct claim about Mary's virginal state after the virginal conception. The tradition, however, developed early.

Whatever else is said about the nature of Mary's virginity, the thing that has to remain prominent in this discussion is the fact that Christ's birth must be affirmed as a real human birth. As we have seen, Ignatius of Antioch, among others, founds his argument for Jesus' real human nature on this fact that he was "truly born." Today official documents repeat the ever-virgin teaching. At the same time, some authors, without wanting to deviate from official teaching, express various opinions about the foundations of this teaching. Others point out that it is not always clear what various statements are intending to affirm at their core. *Lumen Gentium*, for example, says, "This association (between the Mother and the Son) was shown also at the birth of our

Lord, who did not diminish his Mother's virginal purity but sanctified it" (*LG* 57). In the early Church, cultural factors and ascetic ideals identified virtue and virginity. This mindset would naturally find it appropriate to attribute the most virtuous possible state to Mary. One of the questions that faces Christians today is how to understand the core of that early teaching in our culture where marriage is considered a deeply virtuous and ascetically demanding Christian vocation. If Mary is being called a virgin in order to attribute to her ultimate virtue, but present theology no longer perceives a necessary link between *any* sexual activity and an unavoidable sinfulness, how would we want to portray Mary's sinlessness?

Just as there was rather widespread belief quite early on that Mary would not be subjected to original sin, people pondered what follows from that belief. Mary, they reasoned, would not have suffered in childbirth since such suffering was understood from Genesis to be a consequence of Eve's fall from grace. (See Genesis 3:16.)

DOGMA AS CELEBRATION OF GRACE: IMMACULATE CONCEPTION AND ASSUMPTION

The Marian dogmas that were defined most recently, in the nineteenth and twentieth centuries, are unique in the realm of dogmas formally pronounced because they were specifically defined even though no deep threat to Christian belief was at hand. These dogmas arose from pondering Mary's role in the Incarnation and drawing conclusions from this meditation of what would be fitting for God's mother. The dogmas treat the beginning and end of Mary's life and require us to be in touch with the Christian interpretation of the human situation, not only at the beginning and end of an individual life, but the beginning and end point of life itself. The elements of this situation can be labeled the creation (and the fall) and the end times (theologically called the *eschaton*). One could imagine the Christian understanding of these cosmic themes is a ribbon or string that represents history with a beginning and an ending. Even though the two ends of this string are not visible from the current point in history, the community of Christian faith believes that each end is held in the hands of God. The Christian world view is different from that of some nature-based religions that emphasize reality as cyclical—repeating the same patterns over and over in an inevitable round such as that of the seasons. The Christian relationship to God has an element of directional movement through time. This relationship had a beginning and is moving forward toward completion.

From Christian teaching on creation, the beginning, we take the goodness of what exists, God's intention that the world be an orderly place provided with all that human and beasts need to live together in harmony. We take the understanding that humanity, men and women, are created in the image of God, are meant to be companions to one another, and are good. To the extent that the world we experience does not fit that picture, we look to "the fall." Adam and Eve were deceived into thinking that they needed something more than the life that God had provided. Through this choice, they dislodged the created harmony for themselves and their descendents ever after.

Because of the fall, another historical point is located itself on the string. This is the point of redemption, the belief that by a historical event—Christ's Incarnation, life, and death—humanity has been saved from the results of sin. This is a pure gift from a gracious God offered through Jesus and to every person. This is an event of both genuine human history and genuine divine participation. Now God, too, is balancing on the string. Christian belief also encompasses the end toward which this history is traveling. It will be a time of completion and consequences. Human persons will exist in their created completeness—spirit and flesh together. It is also a time of consequences with our preparation judged above all on how we have responded to the needy among us.

Eschatology is the term given to efforts to articulate beliefs about the end of time, about where history is going—either for the individual at death or, more broadly, for creation as we know it. Christian eschatology tells us that God holds both ends of the string—that both the beginning of time and the end of time are in the gracious hands of God. With this faith, a Christian trusts God for the outcome of the individual and communal unknown future. This trust is based on something held in faith—that since the redeeming life, death, and resurrection of Jesus Christ, the community lives a redeemed history moving toward a grace-filled completion. The two Marian dogmas we are considering are basically a reflection of the conviction that Mary was uniquely gifted in the light of her unique role as Jesus' mother. The grace that is offered to each of us was effective in her from the moment of her conception so she was the first of the redeemed. The notion of her privileges is consistent with basic Christian faith because redemption through Christ is at their core. Her privileges are unique because they happen "out of sequence" as the journey of redeemed life is understood to apply to other saved persons.

A Note on the Reformation Critique

In general, the sixteenth century reformers committed themselves to a faith founded only on Scripture. They did, however, honor the early councils of the church that made the foundational pronouncements on the nature of Christ. This included Ephesus with its affirmation that Mary was *Theotokos*. They also kept the ancient creeds including the statement that Christ was "born of the Virgin Mary."

On the other hand, the reformers criticized Roman Catholic understandings of Mary and, *especially*, Catholic devotional practices. Some reformers like Erasmus of Rotterdam expressed critiques from within Roman Catholicism. While he did not reject devotion to Mary in principle, he did object strenuously to much of the way it expressed itself in his day. He complained that this devotion often consisted of fervent prayer to Mary and little or no attention to the most basic Christian morality. He also rejected the widespread spirituality that completely focused on Mary and portrayed Christ in heaven as totally under her control as though he were a child.

Luther had many of the same complaints about exaggerated and superstitious devotional practices. At the same time, he maintained a reverence for Mary for his entire life. His main issue with Marian belief or devotion was with practices or theological positions that in any way diminished the centrality of Christ or the freely given gift of salvation. By the end of his life, he turned away from praying to Mary because, he believed, no one except Christ is a mediator between humanity and God. Luther condemned the Church for practices that made an idol of Mary. He continued to celebrate and preach on the feasts of the Annunciation, the Purification and the Visitation, emphasizing the ways in which they celebrated Christ's Incarnation and de-emphasizing anything that put too much weight on honoring Mary herself. One element of the Reformation reaction to Mary and the saints that Luther repudiated was the widespread practice of destroying devotional paintings and statues.

Later reformers were less inclined to retain any element of Marian devotion. Roman Catholicism responded to Protestant critiques by insisting on their own interpretation of Mary and Marian practice, and belief became a visible sign of division within Christianity. Since Vatican II, a wide variety of Christian denominations as well as Orthodox

Christians are working very actively toward accurately understanding one another and identifying areas of agreement and divergence.

IMMACULATE CONCEPTION

Briefly, this doctrine means that from the very beginning of her existence, Mary was protected from original sin. This belief arose from the respect that people felt should be given to Mary and to Jesus. First of all, it just would not be fitting for Jesus to be born to a person who was touched by sin and, secondly, this protection is something that God would want to do for Mary. The assumption that this was the case seems to have existed long before anyone came up with a suitable theological explanation of how this could be. The great difficulty was partly that early Christians assumed that original sin was passed from one generation to the next through the "lust" that accompanies procreation. This seemed to leave no possibility for Mary to have escaped original sin.

The assumption of Mary's sinlessness first arose from the early practice of celebrating Mary's birth as a feast, when the usual custom was to celebrate a saint's death anniversary. The question this raised was whether it was proper to celebrate an event that included sin—since a person is in sin at birth. This question was raised in the ninth-century but not resolved. The feast continued to be celebrated, while theologians debated whether Mary's complete sinlessness was a privilege that could be theologically justified. The

Franciscan Duns Scotus (1266–1308) eventually provided a way through this theological thicket when he combined Anselm's idea that it was the will rather than the body that transmitted original sin with the idea that God would want to do the "most excellent thing" and could do it. The most excellent thing would be to preserve Mary from sin rather than deliver her from it after the fact.

Mary was redeemed as all of us are by the grace of God, the free, unearned gift of God's love. (See *CCC* 411.) At the same time, Mary consents to God's proposal of her motherhood in a free act. (See *CCC* 428.) In the paradox that Christianity continues to embrace, the gift of God's grace is the foundation of the freedom to make redemptive human choices. In this way, Mary is both privileged and one with the rest of humanity in being redeemed by the grace of Christ—in her case an anticipated redemption.

The immaculate conception has sometimes been preached in a way that emphasizes Mary's privileges at the expense of her human connection with us. Scripture makes us aware that hers was a life that appeared ordinary in every way. She knew grief, joy, and confusion, as well as ordinary day-to-day life. This reminds us that holiness is not found outside our own humanity but within it.

A neglected aspect of this doctrine is the fact that Mary's freedom from original sin should enable us to locate her in deep union with original creation. Rather than being seen as an individual privilege that might isolate Mary from the rest of humanity, could this doctrine be framed to give all humanity new impetus to see resistance to sin as a reunion with original creation in its human and other life forms?

The definitive pronouncement that the immaculate conception is a matter of faith requiring assent came in 1854 by Pope Pius IX in a papal bull (official letter) titled *Ineffabilis Deus*. Even more recently, an additional privilege at the opposite end of Mary's life was officially defined within Roman Catholicism.

THE ASSUMPTION

The assumption speaks to the end of Mary's life at the opposite end of the string of history—still held in the hand of God. Her place in the history of redemption, though, lets the Christian argue that as the person most thoroughly redeemed of all others, she should not face the decay of her body but should immediately experience the resurrection that is the last state of all the redeemed. As noted as early as the third-century, Scripture is completely silent on the end of Mary's life. We have writings from the Greek Father Epiphanius of Salamis (d. 403), in which he examines this question and even wonders if she might have been martyred since Simeon told her that a sword would pierce her soul. (See Luke 2:35.) He concludes that nothing definitive can be known in view of the lack of scriptural evidence. Other early Christian writers like Germanus of Constantinople (d. around 733) argued that Mary would have died, since she was genuinely human and even Jesus himself was not spared death.

The assumption follows from Christian belief in the sinlessness of Mary and the sense that corruption of the body is liked to sin. In addition, Christ's debt of gratitude to her is also cited. The third argument fits most fully with a view of the eschaton as the completion of original creation, with Mary as graced example of redeemed creation.

How do people imagine or image these things if they no longer believe literally in up/down, heaven/hell locations for the eschaton? Note that mental images for these have come from several sources: the highly symbolic literature of the book of Revelation, private revelations to various mystics of various eras, and people's experiences of catastrophic events that seem like they bring at least the local, known world to an end.

A second question to ask about the assumption is about alternative visions of the eschaton. The Old Testament prophets Isaiah and Ezekiel, for example, described the fulfillment of God's will as a time of peace, plenty, harmony, companionship, international unity, and beauty. When history would come to completion, there was flourishing for all: water, food, peace, abundance, healing, and an end to division and violence. How could our understanding of Mary's completed entrance into this time draw others to it? Are there alternatives to her isolated perfection? Could a new imagining of the significance of the assumption teach us to see Mary as a support and inspiration for the difficult and urgent tasks of peacemaking in our time?

VATICAN COUNCIL II

As we shall see in Chapter 3, Marian devotion was always rooted in Mary's significance in Jesus' life and identity. The liturgical feasts of the Church calendar were the earliest expressions of devotion and placed Mary firmly within the cycle of the Church year and the eucharistic celebration. By the time the Second Vatican Council met in 1963, many Marian devotions had sprung up with little or no relationship to Church liturgy. In part, this could be explained by a general distancing of people from understanding and participating fully in the Eucharist. At the same time, there was pressure from some bishops for further emphasis on Mary's privileges through a document solely devoted to her and even, perhaps, a new doctrinal definition around her place in Christ's redemptive work.

The council participants rejected the preparatory document that took this approach, however, and included Mary in the *Dogmatic Constitution on the Church*. In part they wanted to avoid creating ecumenical tensions at a time of outreach and reconciliation with both Orthodox Catholicism and Protestant Christianity. They also had a larger overall program of renewing and emphasizing the liturgy and Scripture. Finally, the council took the tack of re-emphasizing Mary's integral relationship to Christ.

In the Constitution on the Church (*Lumen Gentium*), an entire chapter is devoted to Mary. Catholics are instructed that their reverence for Mary takes place as they are "joined to Christ the head and in communion with all his saints…" (*LG* 52). The document specifically states that there is "but one mediator" who is Christ (*LG* 60). This statement had the effect of setting aside the fears of Protestants and Orthodox Catholics. At the same time, it dashed the hopes of those bishops who had wanted a new declaration of Mary's role in salvation. Devotion to Mary is re-affirmed, especially in the liturgy and approved devotions. "Theologians and preachers" are cautioned against exaggeration in expressing the "special dignity" of Mary and confusing others about the teaching of the Church (*LG* 67). Finally, the significance of Mary is summed up in the ancient affirmation that she is a model or symbol for the Church as it one day hopes to be. As such she is "a sign of certain hope and comfort to the pilgrim People of God" (*LG* 68). In a final paragraph, the bishops appreciatively acknowledge all those who honor Mary, especially Eastern Catholics, who call her Mother of God. Rather than approach Mary in a way that further alienates other Christians, the council ends by asking her to be a heavenly advocate of unity. (See *LG* 423).

Marian belief has never existed in a vacuum but has always interacted with liturgy and devotional practices. As we will see in Chapter 3, the insights and practices of all the baptized, the teaching of specially trained theologians, and the guidance and teaching of Church officials have all given rise to and perpetuated Church teaching through liturgy and everyday devotion. It is these elements of the Christian relationship to Mary that we will take up next.

REFLECTION QUESTIONS

1. *How would you describe your understanding of the basic Marian doctrines? Do you think they are understandable? Spiritually important? Inspiring? Confusing?*

2. *Which elements of Mary's traditional privileges do you find most meaningful and why? How do you relate this element to your lived practice of faith?*

3. *Why does Rahner think that the sinlessness of Mary does not have to separate her from the rest of us? Do you agree? Is his opinion supported by the Gospel of Luke?*

4. *Do you have experience of devotion to Mary before and after Vatican Council II? How would you describe each?*

5. *What has been your experience of dialogue between Protestants and Catholics about the place of Mary in Christian life? Is there someone from a different tradition than yours who you would feel free asking about Mary in their understanding? What do you assume about each other?*

6. *Muslim faith holds Mary in very high esteem. Is there anyone you can ask to share their belief with you? What seems familiar and what is different?*

FOR FURTHER READING

Brown, Peter. *The Body and Society: Men, Women, and Sexual Renunciation in Early Christianity.* New York: Columbia University Press, 1988. Although this is a scholarly work, it is quite readable and very informative for Christians who are interested in the cultural sources of ancient Christian attitudes. Brown cautions that the texts we have available to us from ancient history may reflect ideals rather than actual widespread practice, will concern the ideals and behavior of upper classes rather than the lowly, and are often applied differently to men than to women.

Cunningham, Lawrence S. "The Virgin Mary," *From Trent to Vatican II: Historical and Theological Investigations.* Raymond F. Bulman and Frederick J. Parrella, eds. Oxford: Oxford University Press, 2006.

Gebara, I. and M. Bingemer. *Mary, Mother of God, Mother of the Poor.* Maryknoll, NY: Orbis, 1989. See especially Chapter 4, "Marian Dogmas: Their New Meaning Arising from the Poor and the 'Spirit' of Our Age."

Mary in the Church: A Selection of Teaching Documents. United States Conference of Catholic Bishops. Washington, DC, 2003.

Mary, Mother of God. Braaten, Carl E. and Robert W. Jenson, eds. Grand Rapids, MI: Wm. B. Eerdmans, 2004. This collection of talks from an ecumenical conference gives a window into current thinking about Mary from the point of view of Orthodox, Catholic, and Protestant Christianity.

McBrien, Richard P. *Catholicism.* Revised Edition. San Francisco: HarperOne, 1994. Here you can find a brief but helpful discussion of dogma.

CHAPTER 3
Liturgy, Prayer, and Devotion

When someone dear to us is away, there is no end to the reminders that can bring them vividly to mind: a familiar scent on a sweater in the closet, a song, a favorite food, a turn of phrase, or even an impression too swift to pin down that makes them suddenly present. Our many, rich avenues of connection are part of the complex equipment of being human. These multiple paths into memory and understanding that link us to other people are also some of the ways by which we connect with the sacred in our lives. This is why we cannot draw unyielding boundaries between doctrine and devotion, hymn, or image. This interconnectedness is the source of a very ancient Latin saying in the Church: *lex orandi, lex credendi,* that is, "how we worship reflects our beliefs." This means that the Church's prayer displays the Church's belief or the Church's authentic faith can be recognized by its prayer. As the Church tried to clarify its central beliefs in its early centuries of Christianity, one way to identify authentic belief was to consult the way the Church prayed. We will find in this chapter and the next that what believers hold in faith about Mary can often be mined from their multiple expressions of devotion and from the images that they create and cherish. A few of the ways devotion is expressed are the feasts of the Church, prayers, a commitment to modeling one's life after the object of one's devotion, the creation of images and shrines, and visionary encounters. In this chapter, we will cover feasts, prayer, imitation, and visionary encounters.

EQUIPMENT TO AID IN READING THIS CHAPTER

Quite a bit of the equipment we need for this chapter is already on hand. We will need to recall the information on Eastern and Western Christianity, the development of the various dogmas, and the teachings of Vatican II. We will also need to use the distinction that the Church has made between adoration and veneration.

Adoration and Veneration

From time to time, Christian thinkers have professed nervousness that the honor shown to Mary or to the saints is detracting from or replacing that due to God. This has been settled at least theoretically by making the distinction that adoration is the type of reverence shown to God, and a different category of respect—veneration—as proper to Mary and the saints. While veneration may include prayers of intercession or requests for aid or favors, the link between those of us here in ordinary space and time and those Christians who have gone on ahead of us into eternity, Mary included, is not some form of magic. Rather we are united by the fact that Christ makes us all one; this is a central Christian teaching known as the communion of saints. Those who have been baptized into Christ are forever bonded to each other through Christ. I work at my desk surrounded by concrete treasures that have been given to me by beloved friends. Though these friends are now scattered both here and in eternity, the care that surrounds me continues to be real. This unity is most intensely enacted when the Christian community gathers for Eucharist, which is a memorial that makes present the reality it celebrates. To honor Mary or the saints or to pray to them is to acknowledge our continuing participation together in this enduring bond.

As we have seen, devotion to Mary was not a strong element of early Christian practice. When it began to develop, some people were disturbed by this trend. Admiration might be acceptable, but prayer to Mary seemed to them to put a human person on the same level as God. This was clarified in the early centuries of the Church by using two different Greek words to describe a kind of worship ("adoration" in English) as a fitting response to God, and another type called *doulia* (usually translated "veneration") as the fitting attitude toward saints. Mary is given a unique honor of being designated worthy of *hyperdoulia*, which does not have a common English equivalent, but could be called "super-veneration."

LITURGY, POPULAR DEVOTIONS, POPULAR RELIGION

For now, it is enough to call attention to the fact that a person can be religious or carry on a devotion in a variety of ways. This theme will be developed further below. Liturgy usually refers to the official forms of worship organized and monitored by religious officials. Popular devotions are not called popular because they are the current, trendy favorites, but because they belong to the populace or the people. These are expressions of piety that grow up outside the official worship services. Home shrines, certain kinds of feast day celebrations, and a preference for particular images can all be included. Popular religion is the whole set of attitudes, beliefs, and practices that might relate to a mainstream religion but exist outside usual official promotion. They arise from the customs and needs of the common people.

Though we will only be able to touch on a sampling here, Christians through the ages have expressed their love for the Mother of Christ in a myriad of ways. Ritual, word, and song will be treated in this chapter, and the related topic of images will be taken up in Chapter 4.

HISTORY

It is easy for us to assume that Mary has always been a fixture of central concern in Christianity, but as we saw in Chapter 2, that has not been the case. She appears in early theological arguments, but if one had to identify the figures who inspired devotion from the body of Christians, we would have to point to the martyrs. Their stories were spread; their death anniversaries were celebrated. They were widely admired.

The earliest written prayer to Mary comes to us from an Egyptian manuscript from the third or fourth century and contains phrases that are very familiar to those who use similar words to pray today. It reads: "Under your mercy we take refuge, *Theotokos.* Do not overlook our petitions in adversity, but rescue us from danger, uniquely holy one and uniquely blessed one."* The word "rescue" or deliver is the same as that used in the Our Father. The prayer still in use reads, "We fly to your patronage, O Holy Mother of God. Despise not our petitions in our necessities but deliver us always from all dangers, O glorious and blessed Virgin."

Gregory of Nazianzen, a bishop of Constantinople who died in 390, spoke in one of his sermons about a seemingly widely accepted practice of prayer being addressed to Mary. The account Gregory gives is Justinia, a consecrated virgin who was being seduced by a powerful man, asking the vir-

---

*Price, Richard M. "The Theotokos and the Council of Ephesus," *The Origins of the Cult of the Virgin Mary.* Chris Maunder, ed. London: Burns and Oates, 2008. © Richard M. Price 2008.

gin mother of Jesus to help her. Another Gregory—of Nyssa—who died about 394, reported on the apparition of Mary and the Apostle John to Gregory the Wonderworker (who died around 270). In the midst of serious doctrinal controversies, Mary asked John to enlighten Gregory so that he would be grounded in accurate faith. The biographer seems to take it for granted that such an apparition would make sense to his readers. According to fifth-century Church historian Sozomen, Marian apparitions were common in Gregory of Nazianzen's church. What all this tells us is that at this period—the late fourth century—Christians at least in some locales in the East did not consider prayer to Mary and prayerful interaction with her strange or in need of a great deal of justification.

FEASTS

The earliest celebrated feast that remembers an event in Mary's life seems to come from the church in the East, specifically in Jerusalem, by the middle of the fourth century. Egeria, who made a pilgrimage to Jerusalem in 383, wrote a priceless contemporary report on the liturgical celebrations she witnessed. She mentions a feast of Jesus' Presentation in the Temple celebrated forty days after Epiphany, which would put it in mid-February. Although this was a feast of *Jesus'* presentation, Mary figures prominently in it because of her poignant encounter with Simeon who told her, "a sword will pierce your heart" (Luke 2:35). We know from sermons about this Gospel that preachers used this occasion to ponder various aspects of Marian thought.

There are additional early records of celebrations in the East that honored Mary herself three times during the year. In *Mary the Complete Resource* (2007), Stephen Shoemaker tells us that one celebration was observed two days after Christmas, which was celebrated on December 24 or January 6. Another feast took place on May 15 and the third on August 13. All of these particular observances asked Mary for protection for crops. The first feast devoted exclusively to Mary arose between 417 and 430 and was celebrated in Jerusalem and in Constantinople—the capital of the Eastern empire. This was called "the Virgin's Feast," "the Memory of Mary," or "the Memory of the Theotokos" and celebrated her motherhood and her virginity. In Constantinople, it was celebrated on December 26, and in Jerusalem, on August 15. This Jerusalem feast eventually evolved into the feast that is celebrated on this day today—Mary's Dormition and Assumption. The Dormition is just a way to say "falling asleep," an event that was viewed by some as an actual death and by others as a prelude to the assumption that did not include actual human death. As we saw in Chapter 2, the Roman Catholic Church has not taken an official position on which it was. This shift of focus for the feast of August 15 was probably completed by the mid-sixth century. The option of a votive mass to honor Mary on Saturdays, a practice that is still observed, came into the Roman liturgical calendar by the eleventh century.

By the Middle Ages, this array of feast days was enhanced in the West by imaginative dramas that depicted the events of Mary's life in their human reality. Ordinary people came to feel close to her moments of joy and suffering and to admire her love and courage. You could almost say that she moved from the isolation of privilege to the shared human space of a low Mariology. This shift from emphasis on her universal role in the drama of salvation to her human struggles also encouraged individual people to feel close to her in a personal way. At the same time, she continued to be the beloved ideal of the cloistered monk or nun.

Vatican II, in the Constitution on the Sacred Liturgy (*Sacrosanctum Concilium*), took note of the fact that multiple feasts of saints could overshadow the more central celebrations of the events of Christ's life that shape the cycle of the liturgical year (see 111). For this reason, the general calendar of saints was simplified, and many observances are maintained only in particular places where the celebration is of local cultural or historic importance. Since Vatican II, the list of Marian feasts remaining on the Roman Catholic calendar are the Solemnity of Mary, Mother of God on the octave of Christmas; Our Lady of Lourdes on February 11; the Annunciation on March 25; the Visitation on May 31; the Immaculate Heart of Mary on the Saturday following the Second Sunday after Pentecost; Our Lady of Mount Carmel on July 16; Dedication of Saint Mary Major on August 5; the Assumption on August 15; the Queenship of Mary on

August 23; the Birth of Mary on September 8; Our Lady of Sorrows on September 15; Our Lady of the Rosary on October 7; the Presentation of Mary (in the Temple as a child) on November 21; and the Immaculate Conception on December 8. In the United States, Our Lady of Guadalupe on December 12 is also included.

And what was happening in the Western church all this time? We know that Ambrose (d. 97) was bishop of Milan while it was plagued with fierce disputes over the divinity of Christ. He composed a Christmas hymn for his people that taught them to sing of the virgin birth as a birth that "befitted God." In this way, devotion could also educate in orthodox faith. The major feasts of Mary seem to have appeared in Rome and the West by the mid-seventh century. Specific directions for the celebrations of the feasts of the Annunciation, the Assumption, the Nativity of Mary, and the feast we call [Jesus'] Presentation were given by Pope Sergius I around the end of the seventh century. This tells us that these feasts were already customary by this time. The thirteenth century saw the gradual spread of a feast of the Visitation, and the fourteenth the addition of the Eastern feast of Mary's Presentation.

This last feast, not to be confused with the Presentation of Jesus described in Luke, has as its basis the apocryphal writings that circulated in the early church. They detail how Mary spent her childhood, which included being taken by her parents to the Temple at the age of three. There she lived out her childhood already vowed to virginity. As her work, she spun thread for the weaving a new Temple veil. This is the occupation one sees in many paintings of the annunciation.

As we will see, the image of Mary as a type or metaphor of the Church is developed especially by those widely influential figures of the Western church, Ambrose in Milan and Augustine in North Africa.

TITLES FOR MARY

One doorway into Marian devotion is through the titles or metaphors by which Christians describe and honor her. These are expressed in preaching, teaching, song, and prayer. As we will see, these titles frequently contain an image that also makes them perfect subjects for the creation of art. They are often scriptural, and this is true of the earliest Marian titles which referred to figures and images in the Hebrew bible. These were important to early Christians for proving to critics that they were not an entirely new, upstart religion. Instead, they could show that Christianity was well rooted in the Hebrew Scriptures, which they read as foreshadowing the Christian story.

The earliest title that had been preserved in Christian writing—Mary as the "new Eve"—is of this type. Justin Martyr, who was martyred in 156, referred to Mary by this title. He was not interested in Mary herself, but in showing Jewish critics of Christianity that it had ancient roots in the Hebrew Scriptures. Eve, he argued, was called "mother of all the living" (Genesis 3:20), but since sin came to her offspring through her, the reference to life must have been pointing ahead to Mary. This title was reinforced by the fact that Paul wrote of Christ as the "new Adam."

Sometimes the contrast between Mary and Eve is quite denigrating of Eve; at others it expresses sympathy for her and, according to Saint Iranaeus, represents Mary as an advocate of Eve (*Against the Heresies*). Mary has great compassion for the sufferings of Eve (meaning all the children of Eve) and pleads their case before God. Other writers use the Mary/Eve image to contrast women in general with Mary. Even those baptized and presumed to be saved by Christ are portrayed as dangerous temptresses. Mary, however, is the totally pure ideal. Augustine took pains, though, to assure those who listened to his sermons that both genders (led by the woman, he points out) participated in letting sin into the world. For this reason, God wanted both genders clearly to be assured of their salvation. Furthermore, women are honored by Jesus' being born from a woman and, as Saint Augustine argues, it is impossible for men to blame the woman for earthly mortality (death) or condemn her to eternal damnation (*Sermon 190*).

Early titles for Mary often refer back to the Hebrew Scriptures. "Cedar of Lebanon" and "Ark of the Covenant" are two of these. The cedar of Lebanon appears throughout the Hebrew scriptures as a symbol of strength, beauty, majesty, fertility, God's protection. The Jerusalem Temple was built from Lebanon cedars. "The just shall flourish like the palm tree, shall grow like a cedar of Lebanon. Planted in the house of the Lord, they shall flourish in the courts of our God" (Psalm 92:13–14; see also Psalms 1:3 and 52:10; Jeremiah 17:8.)

The title, Ark of the Covenant (or the New Covenant) refers to the container that the ancient Israelites bore with them from place to place as the resting place for the presence of God until a permanent "house for God" was finally built in Jerusalem. (See Exodus 25:10.) It is obvious that Christians would see Mary in this description. The image also resonates with the account of the annunciation in the Gospel of Luke where "the Holy Spirit overshadowed Mary" as the presence of God had overshadowed the Ark.

"Bride" is another title—Bride who bore God's child— as Church is bride of Jesus. Contemporary Christians are likely to ask, "Is Mary the bride of Christ *and* his mother— which one?" We tend to take our images almost literally in an unhelpful way. This title is a helpful reminder to us of the fact that in most ages of history, images were recognized as just that—imaginative helps to understanding. This allowed them a flexibility and fluidity when using images that people of the scientific age can find quite disconcerting. Medieval Christians, for example, had no problem with a sermon pondering Peter and Paul as the breasts of the church giving it nourishment.

The major theme—*Mary as Church*—originated with Ambrose in the Western church of the late fourth century. Rather than adopting an image from the Hebrew Scriptures to express Christianity's new vision, Ambrose preached Mary as a parallel or symbol of the Church, what theologians call a "type." In looking at Mary, one can see the characteristics of the Church and come to understand and appreciate it better. Some connections include: Mary conceived Christ and gave him his body; she conceives all Christians into the body of Christ, the Church. Speaking of the Christ and the Church, Augustine calls her the "Mother of its Head" and the "Mother of his Members."

Numerous images refer to Mary's virginity. From the Song of Songs come these: "You are an enclosed garden, my sister my bride, an enclosed garden, a fountain sealed" (4:12). When Christian spirituality took a monastic direction in the third and fourth centuries, these images of Enclosed Garden offered the consecrated virgins of monasticism an inspiring model to imitation.

IMITATION

An expression of devotion to Mary that arises especially sharply from the third and fourth centuries on is taking Mary as the model for Christians. This was an age of increasing interest in asceticism, that is, the practice of denying oneself ordinary comforts in pursuit of a religious goal. The age of martyrs had ended with the legalization of Christianity by the emperor Constantine in 313. The new way to express heroic dedication to Christian ideals was asceticism; virginity was the primary expression of this life of self-denial. A description from this period portrays Mary as a young woman before the visit from the angel Gabriel. She lives at home, shut off from contact with strange men, eating and sleeping only out of necessity, and spending her time in prayer. According to this tradition, Mary's admirable life led to her being chosen as Christ's mother.

PRAYER TO MARY

The practice of intercession, or asking Mary for favors, is evident from as early as the fifth century in noncanonical texts devoted to the death of Mary: *Palm of the Tree of Life* and the *Six Books*. Both contain accounts of people receiving miraculous help through their intercession of Mary. The theological background behind this notion is illustrated by a painting that now hangs in the Cloisters in New York and can be viewed on their Web site. It is an early fifteenth century painting called *The Intercession of Christ and the Virgin*, by Lorenzo Monaco of Florence. Intercession or advocate paintings often show small figures around Mary or inside the folds of her cloak. These are the petitioners or those in need of her intercession. In this particular example, Mary and Jesus are large adult figures kneeling on the right and left at the bottom of the canvas. Mary is holding one of her breasts and looking at Jesus, and her words are written on the canvas between them: "Dearest son, because of the milk that I gave you, have mercy on them." With her other hand she gestures to a group of very small figures, the petitioners, kneeling with her and turned toward Christ. Christ, the wounds in his hands clearly showing, gestures with one hand toward Mary and with the other touches the wound in his side. He looks to God in heaven, a figure of the same size as the two below, but surrounded by a glorious ring of stars and golden rays. Christ's words read, "My Father, let those be saved for whom you wished me to suffer the Passion." God gestures toward Jesus, and a relatively small Holy Spirit dove flies down towards him.

This deeply theological work describes the religious thought behind the act of praying to Mary. Any good that comes to humanity comes as the gracious gift of God through the saving life, death, and resurrection of Jesus Christ. Mary stakes a particular claim on Christ because of her intimate relationship of motherhood. The fact that she nursed him is an ancient way of referring to his real humanity, for which he depends on her. The small figures of the petitioners have taken up a place surrounding Mary, but look to Christ for their answer. As Vatican II affirms, "...the Blessed Virgin's salutary influence on men [and women]...flows forth from the superabundance of the merits of Christ, rests on his mediation, depends entirely on it and draws all its power from it" (*Lumen Gentium*, 60). This attitude of looking to Mary for help and protection is a particularly medieval inclination. The wars, plagues, and great schisms of the Church during these times likely weighed heavily on lives of the people. Many felt a deep need for confession and absolution of sins as the idea of

Christ's judgment loomed over them both in sermons and art of the day. Mary's intercession would have given them comfort and hope.

Lay people developed more complex devotional lives with the rise of Mendicant orders. These orders, for example the Franciscans and the Dominicans, were not monks who spent their lives in the monastery. The new orders undertook the mission of preaching both in churches and in the open air. Their sermons were aimed at the laity and often included stories from the legends about Mary and her merciful intervention for sinners.

THE REFORMATION

Christians of the Reformation were especially alert to anything that might in any way lessen the belief that Christ alone is the source of salvation. They saw Catholicism of the Reformation period as seriously distracted from this principle, and this was one of the main points they wanted to reform. Some of the churches that developed out of the Reformation maintained a strong reverence for Mary while rejecting prayer to her. This was Luther's position. A proper prayer to Mary or a saint ought not give the impression that they are in any way able to save of themselves—or even in any way able to mediate the grace that comes from God. Any of this would be a lessening of the principle that Christ is the only mediator. For many of these groups, no form of devotion to Mary or the saints survived.

THE ROSARY

Prayer beads are a part of many religions. Muslims use a set of beads when reciting the ninety-nine Beautiful Names of Allah. Counting beads also show up in the Buddhist recitation of mantras. Prayer beads in Christianity have largely been a devotion of the Western Church and have been used to count prayers for Marian devotions, including the Seven Sorrows of Mary and the rosary. The rosary is the most widespread and seems to have its roots in monastic prayer. Monastic prayer developed a system called the Liturgy of the Hours or the Divine Office, a sung or recited ritual based on the psalms with added Scripture readings and prayers. This was prayed in segments at designated hours throughout a day and was considered the monks' main "work," carried out for the good of the whole Church. The recitation of the hours moved through a cycle that encompassed all of the one hundred fifty psalms. A "little office" dedicated to Mary and including a limited range of psalms had been recited in monasteries since the eighth century and, in medieval times, was also practiced by the laity. This office would only have been available to those who could afford a book or could read, although it was shorter than the Divine Office and would have been easier to memorize.

The rosary was a medieval adaptation of the Hours for people who did not have the time or necessary literacy to undertake the praying of the Hours, which would have been the vast majority of the population. A complete recitation of the rosary with its three sets of mysteries included one hundred fifty recitations of the Hail Mary. In addition, it offered the opportunity to meditate on the central events in the lives of Jesus and Mary. The rosary received papal approval from Pope Alexander VI at the end of the fifteenth century, and it was promoted as a tool to counter the Reformation. Numerous confraternities, which were lay groups dedicated to a particular devotion, grew up for the recitation of the rosary in parishes. While the rosary is thought of as a Marian devotion, the mysteries drew people into the life of Christ. This encouraged a more balanced devotional life than the one-sidedly Marian devotion criticized by the reformers.

POPULAR RELIGION

We sometimes hear of references to popular religion as pursuing particular forms of Marian piety. This is often said of certain ethnic groups or the impoverished majority in a developing nation. Often the impression is given that there is some proper form of religion and then this alternative, more primitive or superstitious form. There is more to the picture than that. Popular religion is a very slippery term that deserves some exploration.

Dutch sociologist Peter Staples has pointed out some very helpful distinctions.* Sometimes "popular" is being

---

*"Official and Popular Religion in an Ecumenical Perspective," *Official and Popular Religion*. Pieter Hendrik Vrijhof and Jacques Waardenburg, eds. The Hague: Mouton Publishers, 1979.

used to label a style of religion as in a "folk" or pre-modern style of religion held by a local population. At other times, "popular" means "non-highbrow," as in popular religious art as opposed to museum pieces or old masters.

An alternative way of talking about "popular" is to consider the closeness or distance between the centers of power and more marginal groups. Every sphere from the family to parish and universal church structures have centers of power and margins. The same person or group may be classified differently depending on their link to the larger institution. A parish pastor, for example, may occupy the center of power in the parish, but the margin of the diocesan Church, especially if the parish lacks prestige. In this model, Staples uses popular religion to designate forms of religious expression at the periphery that are not linked to the local or larger centers of power. A local religious expression that is linked to the institution's centers of power might be called "official" religion.

In some cases, then, even if the style of religion is popular (or non-elite/lowbrow), it may belong to the official sphere. Staples also uses this model to describe the situation in which the periphery maintains what has been core official beliefs, while the center abandons them. This would constitute official religious belief at the margins rather than the center of power. An oppressed group might sing a folk song based on Mary's Magnificat as a prayer of hope for release from injustice—certainly a central Christian aspiration. At the same time, the local hierarchy might be cooperating with the governmental structures of injustice. Recent attempts to give greater respect and validity to local religious practices have the danger of sliding over into a romantic view of popular religious expression as though it is always instinctively wise. Local piety is vulnerable to distortion just as every other expression is. At the same time, a nuanced view that allows for the possibility of genuine expression of central Christian convictions at the center and the margins is most likely to be fruitful. Since there is a wide variety of popular Marian devotion, it is particularly important to consider issues that are too dismissing or that embrace it too quickly.

For Roman Catholics, official religious devotion would begin with the Eucharist, "the source and summit of the Christian life" (*LG* 11). At the other end of the spectrum, we might see a fervent group of people gathered around a Marian image that combines elements of a pre-Christian custom of offerings to crop goddesses and Christian reverence for Mary. Eventually, this image might enter an official liturgical space, or the feast might become part of the official liturgical calendar.

In 2001, the Congregation for Divine Worship in Rome published *Directory on Popular Piety and the Liturgy: Principles and Guidelines*. Besides numerous other mentions of Mary, the entire fifth chapter of the document takes up the topic of Marian devotion with an attitude of encouragement, first of all for its liturgical forms. This is not the end of the matter, however, for "[l]iturgical worship...does not in fact exhaust all the expressive possibilities of the People of God for devotion to the Holy Mother of God." The document affirms that the very poor have a particular devotion to Mary, in part because "[t]hey know that she, like them, was poor, and greatly suffered in meekness and patience."

"OFFICIAL" AND "POPULAR" AFTER VATICAN II

The Second Vatican Council's renewed official emphasis on Scripture and liturgy shifted attention to these spheres in a way that emphasized rational instruction. While devotion to saints and Mary may have lost ground as official religion, popular religion was more likely to maintain these devotions. Sometimes this was done in resentful resistance of anything new, but often, popular devotional habits were directed to purposes that were fully in keeping with the stated goals of Vatican II.

Within official Catholic teaching, both Pope Paul VI and Pope John Paul II issued major statements on Mary. Paul VI's Apostolic Exhortation, *Marialis Cultus* (1974), locates devotion to Mary within Christian worship that "takes its origin and effectiveness from Christ, finds its complete expression in Christ, and leads through Christ in the Spirit to the Father." He describes his purpose in writing as threefold: considering the place of devotion to Mary in relationship to the liturgy, giving direction to the development of devotion, restoring recitation of the rosary. In his section of development of devotion, he makes note of the difficulties some might find in taking Mary as a model when her life and contemporary life, particularly the role of women, are so different.

The encyclical, *Redemptoris Mater,* issued by John Paul II in 1987, is an extended meditation on Mary's journey of faith and the parallel journey of the Church. John Paul also comments on the need for agreement about Mary as part of the union of Christians. He praises the progress and existing agreement of Roman Catholicism and other Christian groups around the Marian doctrines, liturgical prayer, and icon traditions. The encyclical goes on to express a theme that John Paul II especially favored, that of Mary as uniquely sharing in Christ's mediation in the redemption. He is careful to restate in numerous instances the foundational Christian belief that Christ is the one mediator of salvation. This means that it is *through* Christ that God makes salvation available. At the same time, he emphasizes that Mary shares in a special way in that mediation through her total openness to be Christ's mother, for example, and through her suffering with him.

DEVOTION TO MARY OF AND FOR THE POOR

In the years since Vatican II, popular religion and the concerns of those who work with the poor are uniting around devotion to Mary. This devotion is seen as support for liberation from spiritual, cultural, economic, and political oppression. As Archbishop Oscar Romero put it, "the true homage a Christian can pay the Virgin is, like her, to make the effort to incarnate the life of God in the trials of our transitory history" (quoted in *Mary, Mother of God, Mother of the Poor*).

PILGRIMAGE

While international medieval pilgrimage sites like Jerusalem and Rome were highly valued in the piety of the day, there is an obvious lacking in medieval pilgrimage sites for Mary. Her presence was considered universal, and wayside shrines, home icons, parishes, groups, and innumerable monasteries were dedicated to her. Local devotion flourished and was anchored in local images, statues, or relics like Mary's veil, cloak, milk, and hair. Some devotional practices that are used today developed out of the practices of poor people in the Middle Ages. Prayers involving movement like the Stations of the Cross and walking a labyrinth were originally versions of the pilgrimages that drew the wealthy to Jerusalem. The vast majority who were too poor to make the great pilgrimages found an affordable substitute in these practices that could be undertaken in the local church, or at least in a cathedral.

PERSPECTIVES ON APPARITIONS

Apparitions can be thought of as the encounter between a person or group living in present day time and space with a being that is thought of as not occupying present time or space. This being might be a person who has died or a spirit that does not have a body. Throughout the history of Catholic Christianity, encounters with Mary are one of the more frequently reported experiences of this kind. Visionaries usually report both seeing Mary and being able to speak with her.

Among the most familiar Marian apparitions for Catholics of the United States are the apparitions at Guadalupe, Mexico, in 1531; in Lourdes, France, in 1858; and Fatima, Portugal, in 1917. These have all been judged authentic by Church authorities. Ongoing reports of apparitions at Medjugorje, Yugoslavia, have drawn much attention since they began in 1981. This is a case in which official recognition has not been granted but has also not been refused. Lesser known visionary claims that have also been recognized by local or regional bishops are the apparition at Akita, Japan, in 1973; at El-Zeitoun, in Egypt, in 1968; and at Kibeho, Rwanda, in 1981. In these last two appearances, Muslims as well as Christians saw the apparition. The apparitions list above is incomplete and serves only to convey some sense of the breadth of the apparition experience.

OFFICIAL TEACHING

To understand Catholic teaching about apparitions, we have to begin with the Catholic understanding of revelation. Revelation simply means the belief that God's relationship with us includes knowledge that we would be unable to discover completely on our own. Some knowledge about God is considered a natural result of reason. We are capable of learning something of God as creator, for example, from observing the order of the universe. The depth of God's love for us, however, is not something that we could ever come to on our own. God's profound desire to be in relationship to us and the incredible depth of forgiveness that God offers us are not things we would come to through reason. Christians believe that the most complete, ultimate act of revelation is the person Jesus Christ. He is God's definitive revelation. While it is true that understanding and expressing what we know from Jesus is an ongoing process in each era, nothing completely new or contradictory is going to be revealed in the process.

For this reason, even in cases where Church officials might judge that a reported apparition is an authentic supernatural event, no one is obliged to believe its reality or accept the content or message given as definitive revelation. The technical term for these kinds of phenomena is private revelation. The Catechism of the Catholic Church says about private revelation, "It is not their role to improve or complete Christ's definitive Revelation, but to help live more fully by it in a certain period of history. Guided by the Magisterium of the Church, the *sensus fidelium* knows how to discern and welcome in these revelations whatever constitutes an authentic call of Christ or his saints to the Church" (67). Here the *sensus fidelium* means a long-term collective gift of the baptized community that guides it to distinguish what does or does not constitute reliable belief. Each visionary perceives the apparition as he or she is able within the scope of personal natural ability. This, too, might limit the universal acceptance or applicability of a visionary's message. For these reasons, there is never any obligation on the part of believers to affirm the reality of an apparition or the authenticity of its message. This is true even if it has been recognized as authentic by the Church authorities.

CHURCH RECOGNITION

The Church usually leaves the judgment about the authenticity of any apparition to the local bishop. How does a bishop go about assessing such a claim? The first answer is slowly and cautiously. The elements involved in such a judgment are really what one would expect in discerning whether some phenomenon is of God: the availability of sufficient information, compatibly with the Church's doctrinal and moral teaching, and a focus on God rather than the person of the visionary. The rather formal set of criteria held by the Church exists alongside the fact that some apparitions seem to gain recognition on the basis of a long devotional tradition at the site. Particularly if they have not raised doctrinal or moral red flags, they may be places of pilgrimage and devotion for both laity and the hierarchy and so pass into an informal acceptance. Knock in Ireland could be considered an example of this kind of gradual acceptance.

The majority of events that have claimed to be apparitions have never been definitively recognized or rejected. Generally speaking, there is a limit on how much official devotional activity Church officials will encourage at the site of an apparition that has not been recognized, even if it is not disapproved. If there is official affirmation that some genuine supernatural event is taking place, there will be permission for Church sponsored pilgrimages and shrines. Even sites that have not received approval, however, will have an active presence of clergy among groups who arrange their own pilgrimages. This is actually encouraged so that pilgrims have spiritual guidance in their devotional activities, so that the sacraments will be available to them, and so that the Eucharist can play an appropriately central place in the pilgrims' experience.

CONCLUSION

Marian devotion is obviously a topic too vast for a complete treatment in so few pages. To summarize briefly, Marian devotion comes directly out of the Christian understanding of Jesus, particularly the affirmation of his authentic, complete humanity. A mindset of poetry rather than prose would most fully capture the variety of titles by which Christians have honored and appealed to Mary. Devotion to her ranges from the most humble home altar to the great mosaics of the Byzantine churches to the soaring cathedrals of Europe and to the humble Vietnamese shrine dedicated to her ap-

pearance at La-Vang. People identify with her care and ac-
companying presence in every corner of the world and every
social circumstance. Identification with her can support the
strengths and innate dignity of women or can be used to re-
strict them to lives debilitated and endangered by a distort-
ed form of humility. Marian devotion has the marks of the
most ancient notions of the sacred: a force pervasive, strong,
and potentially dangerous. At the same time, though we
may forget it from time to time, Mary is always one like us.

REFLECTION QUESTIONS

1. *Is there anything surprising to you from this chapter?
   What would you like to say back to any of the historical
   or modern figures who portray Mary here?*
2. *Which titles for Mary do you find helpful or appealing?
   Do you have any favorites not mentioned here?*
3. *Are there kinds of devotion to Mary that you find
   unhelpful? Why?*
4. *How do you respond to the monastic ideal of Mary,
   the Virgin?*
5. *How do you understand intercession? Has its role in
   your life changed over your lifetime?*

FOR FURTHER READING

Chiffolo, Anthony F. *100 Names of Mary: Stories and Prayers*. Cincinnati: St. Anthony Messenger Press, 2002. This work combines historical background with traditional and contemporary prayers and is a rich resource for reflection.

Gebara, Ivone and Bingemer, Marie C. *Mary, Mother of God, Mother of the Poor*. Maryknoll, NY: Orbis Books, 1989. (c) 1989 Orbis Books. Used by permission.

Johnson, Elizabeth A. *Friends of God and Prophets: A Feminist Theological Reading of the Communion of Saints*. New York: Continuum, 1999. This exploration of the broader topic of saints sets up a context for thinking about our relationship to Mary.

———. *Truly Our Sister: A Theology of Mary in the Communion of Saints*. New York: Continuum, 2003. This volume gives the larger context for the Scripture passages discussed in Johnson's *Dangerous Memories*.

Spretnak, Charlene. *Missing Mary: The Queen of Heaven and Her Re-emergence in the Modern Church*. New York: Palgrave Macmillan, 2004.

The Essential Mary Handbook: A Summary of Beliefs, Practices, and Prayers. Liguori MO: Liguori Publications, 1999.

CHAPTER 4
Picturing Mary

The Chinese painter He Qi remembers being a young teen in the harsh confinement of a re-education labor camp during China's Cultural Revolution. Because he had artistic skills, he was not forced into the worst of the brutal work of the camp. His daily task was to paint pictures of Chairman Mao. At night, however, he painted an entirely different subject. He had come upon an old magazine picture, a reproduction of "Madonna and Child," by the Italian artist Raphael. Living up until then in an environment entirely permeated with "struggle and hatred," he describes the peace that came to him in the light of the Madonna and Child who seemed to be smiling directly at him. Although he was not yet a Christian, Qi secretly made copies of this picture to give to other inmates of the camp. He wanted to share the peace he had found in those loving faces.

He Qi's story describes a most unusual setting for beginning a relationship with Mary. What he has in common with many others, however, is the fact that his bond with Mary is deeply influenced by images. This reality has been reinforced for me from the beginning of this book project. Friends, colleagues, and strangers have brought me their favorite pictures. A woman I met at a professional meeting went back to her hotel room to bring me a card that she had received at a funeral home in Miami. She was touched by this particular icon of Mary, because she felt that Mary's sorrowful face reflects the truth about the loss of a loved one. A friend called excitedly from a vacation trip halfway across the country. She had seen a statue of pregnant Mary and would send me a photo.

Just as artistic depictions can attract people to Mary, the reverse is also true. Some people feel distant from Mary because they cannot identify with the appearance of perpetual youth, the innocence, the slender body, or the isolated perfection of her images. Others reject images that draw attention to Mary's pregnant body or peasant origins. These positive and negative reactions bear witness to the fact that images have the power to speak to aspects of human experience that are emotionally embedded. We might agree *intellectually*, for example, with the fact that Mary was a fully human woman, but *seeing* her portrayed as obviously female might be discomforting. This is partly because gender expectations are so deeply and often unconsciously rooted in a group's way of life. Statues or paintings of Mary do not stand alone or arise from nowhere, but often express the ideals of appearance and behavior that a particular society requires for women. For all of these reasons, we can expect intense responses to the wide variety of Marian images.

It is certainly true that most Christians have received their notion of Mary from pictures, hymns, preaching, and devotions rather than through study or reading. The Christian tradition can boast a broad and deep range of images of Mary, most of which are unfamiliar to today's Christian. We will be looking here at a broad range of traditions to get an idea of what has been important to past generations. We will also look at the way that many images have been imbued with a complex theology and how they might enrich our understanding of Mary today.

Because, as we have seen, Mary's place in Christian belief is so complex, it takes multiple images to convey the fullness of her tradition. In this chapter, we will explore some of the history and variety of these numerous images. We will get a sense of the theological symbols in familiar Marian images. We will also see what can be learned from some images that are unfamiliar to most people today. Depictions of Mary have changed with changing understandings of holiness and with changing convictions about how God deals with the human family. When we learn to read them, pictures and statues from previous centuries can convey a very complex and instructive Mariology.

For a variety of reasons, many Catholics growing up in the United States in the last century have grown up with a very limited range of available Marian images. The exception to this would be those who have a strong ethnic identity that claims a particular representation of Mary. In most public settings, images have tended to be of a type that picture Mary alone, as Caucasian, with a slender, very young, idealized body, and with a posture and expression that convey humility and submissive obedience. Occasionally she is pictured with her child or as part of a Holy Family trio. Often these imagine a very limited identity for Mary, for women, and for Christians. In this chapter, we will look at a broader range of images from Christian history. Fortunately these are readily available on the Internet where one can find all those referred to here and many more.

We will be looking at images that come from Orthodox (Eastern) and Western Catholicism. We will see some that represent the ways that Mary is unique and privileged. Other images will be more representative of Mary as she shares a common humanity with us. We will also notice the way culture reflects Mary and Mary acts back on culture. This is to say we may unconsciously form our image of the Virgin Mary in relation to what we value and from our own experiences, just as people have done throughout the ages. With this in mind, we might ask of each image we meet: "What ideals about women are being depicted, and how are they related to the cultural expectations of Christians and of women? A fascinating illustration of our individual views of Mary can be found by calling up Internet images labeled, "Virgin Mary Planters." These planters represent a type of image especially common in Catholic homes and classrooms in the United States in the mid-twentieth century. On viewing these images, one might ask: What ideals about Mary are being depicted? What relationship do these ideals have to the cultural expectations of Catholic women of the 1950s? These types of questions are relevant for images developed in any century.

EQUIPMENT TO AID IN READING THIS CHAPTER

Having access to the Internet for this chapter will help bring a fuller appreciation of the images we will explore. And, of course, these images are widely available in public libraries. The only other equipment needed is a curious mind to receive the wide range of ways that Christians through the centuries have expressed a sense of Mary and her significance. It is certainly true that most Christians have received their notion of Mary from stories, Scripture, pictures, hymns, preaching, and devotions rather than through detailed study. The Christian tradition can boast a broad and deep range of images of Mary, most of which are unfamiliar to today's Christian. We will be looking here at a broad range of traditions to get an idea of what has been important to past generations. We will also look at the way that many images have been imbued with a complex theology and how they might enrich our understanding of Mary today.

It will also be helpful to recall our earlier encounters with *apocryphal* or noncanonical gospels. These early writings never made it into the *canon*—the officially accepted list of books of Christian Scripture. Nonetheless, they were frequently treated as authoritative. The pious as well as preachers and artists called on them to illuminate aspects of the lives of Jesus, the disciples, and Mary, about which the canonical Gospels are silent.

A new term in this chapter is *Byzantine*, which is applied to the art of the Eastern Church. The beauty and variety of these mosaics and painted panels is without equal.

PICTURING MARY

Historically, major sources for Marian images have been Scripture and several apocryphal works, especially the *Protevangelium of James,* which fleshed out her early life. Much of what appeared in art about Mary's death can be found in the thirteenth-century collection of readings on the saints that came to be called the *Golden Legend.* This was a kind of compilation of popular saints' stories with reflections for feasts, saints' days, and seasons of the Church calendar. The collection included extensive descriptions of Mary's life and death. Other resources for Marian art have been indigenous religions in areas that converted to Christianity. Existing ideas of how sacred persons would appear and how they might assist in a person's or community's needs naturally influenced a people's embodiment of Christianity.

Encounters with images of Mary demonstrate that no image stands alone in some space outside human history. Images of Mary come out of particular historical, cultural, and theological locations and are adopted into a wide variety of other locations. An "image" of Mary may be an actual visual depiction in painting, sculpture, tapestry, plastic, toast, or rust, to name but a few of the media in which believers have depicted or discovered her. One might also name as an image a person's particular way of holding Mary in her or his imagination. Included in one's image of Mary might be her relationship to self, humanity, the created world, Christ, God, Church, the universe, or the world beyond earthly death.

BASIC THEOLOGICAL ORIENTATIONS

Two of Mary's privileges will appear very often in both subtle and explicit ways across many styles of art and centuries of belief and devotion. Learning to read them will help us make deeper sense of familiar and unfamiliar portrayals. Two particularly relevant attributes are Mary's freedom from original sin and her virginity. Her freedom from original sin, while not officially declared a dogma until 1954, did give rise to both debates and assumptions about what this would mean. Some believed that she was free from the consequences that the book of Genesis listed as results of Adam and Eve's disobedience. (See Genesis 3:16–19.) This meant that Mary, unlike other women, must not have experienced pain in childbirth. This belief affected artistic depictions of the birth of Jesus.

Other human experiences like the bodily weaknesses of old age and death were presumed to be consequences of original sin and so not applicable to Mary. This belief is reflected in the fact that artists seldom pictured Mary as aging. It also influenced depictions of Mary's death. In some cases, depictions of her death show her being assumed into heaven, but leaving ambiguous the issue of whether she actually experienced death. Artists have also expressed Mary's sinlessness or *spiritual* perfection by giving her an appearance of *physical* perfection according to the standards of female beauty of their own age.

Belief in Mary's perpetual virginity was expressed in art by images that give her the attributes of an unmarried woman—even after her marriage. This was expressed differently in different cultures. In some places, for example, unmarried girls wore their hair long and unbound while married women wore their hair in braids or a bun and covered by a cap. In this case, Mary, even as a married woman, might continue to be pictured with her hair unbound. Depicting Mary as extremely young, barely mature, is another method of visually referring to virginity.

MARY'S SUFFERING

The theme of Mary's suffering has also made a frequent appearance in implicit and explicit forms. This can appear as a somber expression on her face while she is holding her child. This expresses her awareness of his coming suffering, often as a visual reference back to the prophecy of Simeon at the presentation of Jesus in the Temple. "Behold, this child is destined for the fall and rise of many in Israel, and to be a sign that will be contradicted (and you yourself a sword will pierce) so that the thoughts of many hearts may be revealed" (Luke 2:34–35). A large variety of symbols can appear along with the mother and child: a cross in a distant landscape, an angel holding nails or a crown of thorns, or a rooster signaling Jesus' betrayal. These are not intended to be depressing, but to remind the viewer that salvation is the ultimate outcome of this child's birth and of this mother's childbearing.

Art historian Amy Neff suggests that some medieval depictions of Mary at the foot of the cross are explicit references to a belief that the pain she did not experience in childbirth was hers at the cross. Here Mary helped to give birth to salvation. A fine example of this type of portrayal of Mary is seen in the "Seven Sacraments Altarpiece" by the Flemish painter, Rogier van der Weyden. Neff makes her case based on the parallels that can be seen between medieval pictures of the postures of women being supported during childbirth and the posture of the swooning Mary under the cross.

Perception of Mary's suffering vary with historical period and culture. Some Medieval and Renaissance witnesses to depictions of Mary's suffering may have interpreted it in ways that we might not immediately recognize. Mary at the foot of the cross was not only grieving for the suffering and death of her son. People from those centuries would also have been very aware of her concrete financial insecurity as her only child died before her. A small family was a sign of poverty, since harsh living conditions contributed to higher rate of infant mortality. Children were part of the family workforce and also an elderly parent's only source of care. A widow without children would have been in a most precarious state of affairs. Mary nursing her own child would also have spoken of her poverty, since wealthy women commonly hired someone to nurse their children.

In a similar way, poor and oppressed persons in Latin American rely on Mary as someone whose son was unjustly executed. In her suffering, she understands and sympathizes with the suffering of poor mothers. She accepts and loves them when they have no one else.

EARLIEST ROMAN IMAGE IN THE CATACOMBS

The earliest days of the Roman and Western church are almost bereft of images because of the persecution of Christians. Christianity had no public gathering spaces. There are some ancient images in the catacombs where Christians met in secret, but the images tend to be damaged or restored by people with a firm idea of what they "ought to" portray. In the Catacomb of Priscilla outside Rome, we find an image of a mother and child in an ancient fresco painted about 230 AD. A sketch of the fresco appears on the web page of the International Early Mariology Project (http://www.cecs. acu.edu/au/mariologyproject.htm). These images often lay claim as the earliest evidence of devotion to Mary. More recent analysis, however, casts doubt on this assumption and proposes that it is likely to be a customary image of the occupants of the adjacent tomb. Other similar ambiguous images that were often assumed to be Mary and her child are being rethought as images of the Church. At least a few historians propose that the mosaics of Mary in St. Mary Major, built around 431, are probably the earliest Roman pictorial evidence of devotion to Mary.

EARLY EASTERN IMAGES

In Eastern Christianity, early images of Mary were not considered self-expressions of the painter or totally passive material objects. Mary was present where the icon was present, and many were credited with miracles. This understanding of icons was supported by the tradition that the Gospel writer Luke had painted the first icon of Mary, which faithfully represented her. This tradition valued subsequent paintings, not for their originality, but for their fidelity to the original image.

Devotion to Mary did not begin when she was pronounced Mother of God (*Theotokos*) at the council at Ephesus in 431. After the council, though, there was less argument about the legitimacy of veneration of Mary. It was almost as if a door had opened to more devotion and devotional depictions. Almost no pictures of Mary from this period are available to us, however, because of the iconoclast (image-breaking) dispute that broke out in the Eastern region of the Church for long periods between 726 and 843. During iconoclastic periods, the making and devotional use of images of Christ and the saints, including Mary, were forbidden; such images were actively destroyed. Christians at this time were living in a world that encompassed the classical Greek appreciation for beauty and art and, at the same time, the Jewish and Muslim rejection of images as polytheistic idols. In addition to these influences, Hans Belting includes these elements among the mix of factors that were involved at one time or another: economics, various military factions, a desire to unite the empire without the divisive effects of local loyalties, power struggles between monks and emperors, and social class divisions.

The basis of this crisis is clear if we keep in mind the understanding of images that prevailed at the time. Believers of those centuries experienced icons as making present the person portrayed. Icons were not just art works to be admired, owned, sold, and displayed. They were personal presences. This makes it understandable, for example, that an emperor who thought of *himself* as the representative of God within the empire, would want to have the icon of Christ removed from his palace facade. At the same time, a monastery or church that claimed a revered icon could count on a measure of religious and political power.

John Damascene, who died about 750 and whose sermons and writings show a great love of Mary, defended the use of icons. In his view, no icon could picture God, but they could represent Christ as the Incarnate Word. He argued that Mary and the saints were also suitable subjects for icons. The believer honored the person represented, rather than the wood or the paint. It is helpful to remember here that Mary played an important role in the early church as the grounding for the true humanity of Christ.

A council at Nicaea in 787 restored the use of icons by arguing that the Incarnation had brought the Divine into matter, and so images of Christ merely continued that Incarnation. This breakthrough proved to be a temporary pause in the dispute, which only ended with a synod at Constantinople in 843. Even after icons were accepted, norms were established to protect against the possibility that something like an idol might be created. Standards developed that restricted images to being flat (rather than sculptured), to following a particular tradition of proportions (rather than seeking realism), and to using a narrow range of colors with symbolic meanings. These directives give the icons of Orthodox (Eastern) Christianity their distinctive appearance. It also explains why we see no sculpture in Eastern depictions of Mary, though such depictions will be very common in the West.

MARY IN BYZANTINE ART

Mary: Art, Culture, and Religion through the Ages, described in the resources at the end of this chapter, has a well-illustrated chapter on Byzantine images. In the East, images of Mary regularly appeared in mosaics, wall paintings, and in painted wood panels. Much of the earliest works were destroyed in several periods of iconoclasm. Very early images from the sixth century can still be seen in churches in Cyprus. Striking images in Venice and Ravenna (Italian cities today) are counted among the Byzantine contribution because these were originally Byzantine colonies. In the great church of Hagia Sophia, in Istanbul (formerly Constantinople), one majestic ceiling mosaic shows Mary enthroned and holding Jesus. This will become a very common pose. Another unique mosaic shows her being offered the Hagia Sophia church and the royal city from two emperors. Other churches show her standing alone with her hands in the orans position—raised on either side of her in a traditional position of prayer. She also appears in the dress of an empress. Scenes from Mary's life became the subject of church decoration.

Byzantine paintings on panels of wood—either as church decorations or for private devotion—have produced a set of traditional images, such as Mary in a tender embrace with the child. Mary nursing the child is another common image. Images showing Mary in a stance of prayer and the Christ child within a circular or oval medallion in the center of her body referred to her carrying Christ in her womb. Byzantine icon painters did not seek novelty or self-expression but, rather, valued fidelity to the prayerful reproduction of traditional forms. This did not stop a multiplicity of images from developing, some of them claiming miraculous origins. A search for "wonder-working icons" will turn up an amazing array of beautiful paintings with explanations.

WESTERN IMAGES

The Western Church was deeply influenced by icon forms and styles but had a different approach to religious art. Some, like the Carolingian King Charlemagne, resisted the decrees of the council at Nicaea. Others, including the popes, accepted Nicaea in its basic outline. Differences of opinion in the West did not create the crisis it had in the East, but led to a two-part teaching that left the door open for a variety of images to flourish. Worship or even veneration of an image was rejected. At the same time, the Church affirmed the educational benefit of pictures, especially for the illiterate. Use of images to beautify a church was also permissible. The official Roman position on iconoclasm was worked out at the Council of Frankfurt in 794.

In the West, there was no prescribed form for images as there was in the East, so statues were permitted and grew into general acceptability by the twelfth century. Many of the statues that first appeared in the West were images of the saints. These were constructed to form a case for a small

relic from the body of the saint. Emphasis was on veneration of the relic, which had been common since the days of
the early Christian martyrs. Depictions of Jesus were typi-
cally in the form of the crucifix or statues of Christ seated on
Mary's lap. Mary does not appear alone, but is usually seated
on an impressive throne where she in turn forms a throne
for Christ on her lap.

In the Middle Ages, paintings that were created as large
altar decorations drew on elements of Mary's life story.
Events commonly portrayed included many from the *Protevangelium of James* such as her conception, birth, upbring-
ing in the Temple, and betrothal to Joseph. Other sources
were the Gospels of Luke and Matthew, which provided
accounts of Jesus' conception and early life including the
annunciation, visitation, nativity, and presentation in the
Temple. In addition to the events of Mary's early life depicted in the *Protevangelium of James*, other apocryphal works
provided detailed accounts of Mary's death. The *Obsequies
of the Virgin* and the set of traditions known as the *Six Books*
are among works from as early as the fifth century that professed to contain reports of the events surrounding Mary's
death. These were also popular in devotional paintings commissioned for the prayer and meditation of individuals. This
period contributed the image of Mary sheltering petitioners
in a vast cloak. In this form, she is named "Our Lady of Refuge" or "Madonna of the Mantle."

Images of Mary became a contentious subject at the time
of the Reformation. The reformers particularly objected to

the title Queen of Heaven for two reasons. First, they argued that it elevated Mary to a rank that only belongs to Christ. Second, the reformers emphasized Scripture as the sole source of revelation and did not find any scriptural basis for applying the title of queen to Mary. This contrasted with Roman Catholic teaching that also gives a place to the tradition of the Church as a source of religious truth. Of course, this is not meant to supercede or contradict anything found in Scripture.

As the Catholic Church took up its own reforms, its insistence on the importance and majesty of Mary and the promotion of queenly images was one way to assert that position. Pope Urban VIII carried out a project that perfectly illustrates this policy when he directed that gold crowns or elaborate halos be added to the countless Marian paintings of Rome. This controversy over the theology conveyed by images is just one of many that have taken place over the centuries.

IMAGES AS THEOLOGY

While Christians agree that Mary is both unique and a fully, genuinely human person, a noticeable tension can sometimes be detected between her solidarity with humanity and the understanding that she is remarkably privileged. In contemporary times, the watercolorist Julie Vivas has illustrated the nativity story in a book of that name. One can see the nature of her earthy illustrations by accessing images of the book on the Internet. Customer reviews reveal a full spectrum of reader opinions. Some readers delight in its human reality and promise to buy the book for everyone they know. At the other end of the scale are those who say that they would never give it to their children, because to do so would destroy a respect for God and Mary that the reviewer has worked to instill. These split reactions are not limited to popular works or to our own day.

Arguments over the proper way to portray Mary are of interest because they expose assumptions, values, and convictions that might not otherwise surface. Often the underlying disagreement is really about Mary's relationship to the human and to the sacred, or about the socially acceptable way to view women's roles and their bodies. A clear illustration of this is the seventeenth-century controversy over a painting by Michelangelo Caravaggio called "Death of the Virgin." Examining this painting in some detail offers an opportunity to appreciate the complex theological statement that can be expressed in what appear to be rather simple paintings of a familiar subject. Such an analysis could be done for portrayals of many familiar scenes.

Caravaggio's "Death of the Virgin" is a very large painting standing almost thirteen feet tall and eight feet wide, which makes the painted figures almost life-size. The historical record is not entirely clear, but it seems that the painting was finished in a timely manner and hung in its intended place, but by 1607, it had been removed and sold. A second artist, Carlo Saraceni, a friend of Caravaggio, was then commissioned to paint the same subject, and that work was also rejected. Saraceni finally painted yet another version of the same scene that was deemed acceptable, and this is the work that hangs in the church today.

The scene Caravaggio was asked to paint is not contained in the Gospels, but descriptions of it were widely available in a number of apocryphal accounts. A particularly popular source was *Golden Legend* by the thirteenth-century Italian Dominican, Jacobus De Voragine. The book is a set of readings (the contemporary meaning of "legend" in the title) that covers the feasts of the Church calendar and includes a detailed description of Mary's death and assumption. By the late seventh-century, Eastern depictions of Mary's death had developed into a fairly standard set of figures and postures, and these spread into the West. By Caravaggio's day, theologians seemed well aware that the accounts were legends rather than Gospel tradition, but this did nothing to stop their being spread through popular preaching and in art. What was in these accounts?

According to the *Golden Legend*, the tradition about Mary's death is attributed to John the Evangelist in an apocryphal account. Some of the details of the account include the annunciation to Mary by an angel of her coming death in three days, and her wish to have the Apostles present for her death and burial. This desire is fulfilled when the Apostles are all "plucked up" from wherever they are and brought to Mary's dwelling. There follows an elaborate scene in which Christ and Mary sing responses to one another, and her soul goes out of her body into Christ's arms. An extended description of her funeral procession and a three-day wake ends with Christ coming to take her body to heaven. Searching "Death of the Virgin" on the Internet will turn up ample examples of how elaborately this account was generally portrayed with ranks of Apostles, angels, and candles. Christ holds Mary's soul in the shape of an infant or waits in heaven to enthrone and crown her. The emphasis is clearly on Mary's privileges and, indeed, Jacobus situations this reading on August 15, which is celebrated as the feast of the Assumption.

How did Caravaggio depict the scene? There are no angels, blessed candles, holy books, no flowers, no crown waiting in heaven, no image of her soul in Christ's arms or her body ascending into heaven. There is the faintest of halos behind Mary's head, and that is the extent of conventional religious imagery. In his painting, Mary looks like a dead woman with swollen ankles. Beside her, Caravaggio prominently features an unconventional figure, Mary Magdalen, who seldom appears in the legendary scenes. She has apparently been washing Mary's body and has been overcome with grief. Her wash basin occupies the foreground of the painting. Peter stands at Mary's feet with his own bare feet exposed next to the basin. Mary lies with one arm extended, the other at her side under her right breast, and her head to one side.

Interpretations of the painting have suggested that the painting presents a profound theological statement. The artist displays his theology, not through obvious religious symbols, but through the bodies and surroundings of his figures and the other religious imagery that would have been familiar to his viewers. Caravaggio's theology is deeply incarnational, that is, within the very ordinary scene of friends gathered in mourning rather than in additional religious symbols added to the scene. This fact shows God's work is being done in the ordinary human events of life.

On its surface, the painting is entirely low Mariology; she is shown in her simple humanity. On another level, however, this simple humanity includes a sharing in the redemptive death of Christ. The position of Mary's dead body echoes that of Christ as he is depicted after being taken down from the cross. Her hand resting on her side touches the place where the spear pierced Jesus' side. Her pose also echoes some depictions of her suffering at Christ's death where she appears to have undergone a death of her own. The scene also echoes with a complex interplay of the Gospel themes of repentance, forgiveness, and service. The basin which Mary Magdalen has been using to wash Mary's body resonates with the Gospel story of Jesus washing Peter's feet at the Last Supper very shortly before Peter would betray him. (See John 13:3–11.) In another Gospel account, a sinful woman, traditionally but mistakenly assumed to be Mary Magdalen, washed Jesus' feet with her tears and anointed them with costly perfume. (See Matthew 26:6–13; Mark 14:3–9; Luke 7:36–50.)

EXPLORING UNFAMILIAR IMAGES

Some types of Marian images that were familiar to Christians in past centuries are quite unfamiliar to us today. Some of them are particularly helpful for keeping us in touch with Mary's human reality and with the fact that her body was real. This can be a valuable balance to images that emphasize spiritual perfection and that can make her seem rather distant or detached from her body. Medieval and renaissance paintings regularly pictured Mary nursing her child. Many find these tender portraits naturally appealing; they also contain an essential theological message about Christ. They refer back to the oldest theological reflections on Mary that call on her humanity as evidence that Christ is truly human. He was gestated and nourished as any human child must be. Such images can be found under a number of titles including *Maria Lactans* and "Our Lady of Milk and Safe Delivery." Residents of St. Augustine, Florida, have honored her under the later title, which shows Mary pregnant, since the early part of the eighteenth century. Other works honor her pregnancy under the title, "Our Lady of the Expectation."

Equally unfamiliar to most contemporary Catholics is the ancient tradition of Mary as advocate in which she reminds Christ of the fact that she nursed him, and so he should now listen to her pleas on behalf of those for whom she intercedes. One of many painting of this type, "The Intercession of Christ and the Virgin," an early fifteenth-century work by Lorenzo Monaco, hangs in the Cloisters Museum in New York City. It shows Christ and Mary kneeling before God with a group of small figures between them. These people pray to Christ while Mary, showing one of her breasts says, "Dearest son, because of the milk that I gave you, have mercy on them." Jesus in turn shows the wound in his side and says, "My Father, let those be saved for whom you wished me to suffer the Passion."

Since the Medieval era, traditions of Mary as a protector of crops and an advocate for agricultural fertility have been common. Sometimes she is pictured with sheaves of grain. This is common in the "Mother of God, Grower of Crops" icons. In the Western tradition, she is sometimes pictured with stalks of grain on her robe or as an illustration of legends about miraculous growth of crops. Much has been made of the fact that there is overlap between these traditions and images and those of various "grain goddesses." Official rejection of various "pagan" rites and personages left a vacuum where the desperate concerns of ordinary people had been expressed. Mary filled that vacuum as the one who has time for the ordinary concerns of ordinary people.

An additional category of unfamiliar images includes those contemporary images that express ethnic diversity. People whose heritage is European are likely to be uncritical of the fact that no one in Jesus' world really looked like the classical religious pictures that are most commonly viewed and used for private devotion or the decoration of liturgical spaces. It remains true, however, that the rarest of images are those that could conceivably have come from Jesus' homeland.

FAMILIAR IMAGES

Images that are relatively familiar to most of us are those depicting Mary in her immaculate conception and her assumption. Other familiar pictures belong to a group called "Black Madonnas." These would include a number of pilgrimage images from Europe including "Our Lady of Czestochowa" and "Our Lady of Perpetual Help." "Our Lady of Guadalupe," *la Morenita* (little dark one), rounds out our sample of images that are currently widely available.

IMMACULATE CONCEPTION

As we have seen, this doctrine describes Mary's freedom from original sin from her conception as a favor granted to her in anticipation of the saving work of Christ. The Church in its worship and prayer and in theological reflection and artistic expression explored this doctrine long before its definition as a dogma in 1854. The earliest artistic renderings, which are quite foreign to most of us today, took their content from the apocryphal *Protevangelium of James*. This noncanonical source says that an angel told each of Mary's parents separately that they were to have a child. Anne and Joachim set off to tell each other the news and met at the

Golden Gate of the Jerusalem Temple. This meeting was the earliest way that the immaculate conception was pictured. Another early tradition showed Mary's mother with an infant visible in her womb.

Gradually—certainly after the Reformation—these traditions gave way to scenes that are more familiar today. In the middle of the seventeenth-century, the Spanish painter and commentator on art, Francisco Pachero, wrote a prescription for ideal paintings of the immaculate conception. He recommended that Mary be young—twelve or thirteen—with a glowing aura around her body, twelve stars around her head, and the moon under her feet. The stars and moon refer back to the woman in the book of Revelation "clothed with the sun, with the moon under her feet, and on her head a crown of twelve stars." This woman is in the process of giving birth, but she is pursued by a great dragon. She succeeds in giving birth to her child, who is rescued by God while she herself is sheltered by God in the desert. (See Revelation 12: 1–3.) Although the woman has been interpreted variously as Israel, the Church, or Mary, the pictorial elements have become firmly fixed as Marian symbols.

Images of the immaculate conception have also been influenced by an apparition of Mary to French novice, Catherine Labouré (1806–1857). The spread of this image as "the Miraculous Medal" made this one of the most familiar of Marian images today. Catherine described Mary as standing on a globe with a snake under her feet. This is generally interpreted as a defeat of evil from the Genesis account of the fall and its consequences. God says to the serpent in Genesis, "I will put enmity between you and the woman, and between your offspring and hers; he will strike your head, while you strike his heel" (Genesis 3:15). The serpent came to be linked to Mary because the Latin Vulgate translation of Genesis, which was used for Catholic Bibles, mistakenly had the translation as "she will strike your head..."

ASSUMPTION

Byzantine depictions of the assumption usually focused on Mary's *dormition* or "falling asleep." The tradition included the later finding of her empty tomb, but the Western image of Mary's body rising from earth are not known in the Byzantine tradition. As we have seen, the death of the Virgin was widely depicted—always with the belief that she would be assumed. Such scenes are seldom part of contemporary art, which has been taken over by the depiction of Mary being borne bodily into heaven on clouds with the accompaniment or assistance of angels. Sometimes Jesus or the Trinity can be seen awaiting her, often with a crown.

OUR LADY OF GUADALUPE

This embodiment of Mary is known affectionately in Spanish as *la Morenita* ("little dark one"). In 1946, Pope Pius XII declared Our Lady of Guadalupe the Patroness of the Americas. Discussion continues over whether her cult is a way of protecting and honoring indigenous Mexican peoples or whether it is a way of absorbing and suppressing these cultures. Contemporary artists continue to reflect on this image and its significance. For two very different contemporary visions of the Virgin of Guadalupe, see the work of Michael Walker and Yolanda López. López openly rejects what she sees as the passive stance that the traditional image encourages in women.

SOME CONCERNS

Wrapping up this short tour of an endlessly rich subject are a couple of contemporary concerns. The majority of images of Mary are intent on showing her virtue and sinlessness. They adopt some form of the current culturally ideal woman to symbolize her moral perfection. As we saw in Chapter 3, this perfection can be interpreted to include cultural roles of submission and obedience that are not religious ideals for adult women. In addition, Mary has not traditionally been shown aging or sick because of the assumption that her immaculate conception would have freed her from these sufferings.

REFLECTION QUESTIONS

1. *What are your preferred images of Mary? Are there some that make you uneasy or challenge you? What convictions or feelings about Mary give rise to these preferences?*

2. *Are there any aspects of your ideas or feelings about Mary that you do not usually (or ever) find represented in the available images?*

3. *Does anything surprise you about images from former centuries? Are there any you would add?*

4. *Have you seen any images of Mary that make it clear that she was a Middle Eastern woman? How do you think such images would be received?*

5. *Are there aspects of Mary's life that are not available to us in contemporary images?*

FOR FURTHER READING

Ebertshäuser, Caroline H., Herbert Haag, Joe H. Kirchberger, and Dorothee Sölle. *Mary: Art, Culture, and Religion through the Ages.* Translated by Peter Heinegg. New York: Crossroad Publishing, 1998. This is a wonderful combination of informative and reflective text and lovely pictures from every era and style. It is relatively inexpensive for a book of its kind.

Divine Mirrors: The Virgin Mary in the Visual Arts. Melissa R. Katz, ed. New York: Oxford University Press, 2001.

McBride, O., Alfred Praem. *Images of Mary.* Cincinnati, OH: St. Anthony Messenger Press, 1998.

Neff, Amy. "The Pain of Compassion: Mary's Labor at the Foot of the Cross," *Art Bulletin* 53, no. 2 (June 1998): 254–273.

Parlby, Geri. "The Origins of Marian Art in the Catacombs and the Problems of Identification," *The Origins of the Cult of the Virgin Mary.* Chris Maunder, ed. London: Burns and Oates, 2008.

Rodriguez, Jeanette. *Stories We Live: Cuentos Que Vivimos: Hispanic Women's Spirituality,* 1996 Madeleva Lecture. Mahwah, NJ: Paulist Press, 1996. The author of this small volume offers theological reflections and first person accounts of the significance of the Guadalupe appearance and the ongoing stories and visions of Latina women.

Vivas, Julie. *The Nativity.* New York: Houghton Mifflin Harcourt, 2006.

CHAPTER 5
Thoughts for the Way Ahead

Having explored together some of the rich Marian tradition of devotions, doctrine, practices, texts, and images, we conclude with a brief consideration of two areas of contemporary development. These are areas where Marian teaching and devotion might fruitfully develop during the next generation.

MARY AND SHARED DEVOTION

As we saw in Chapter 3, visionary encounters with Mary have been reported on almost every continent. Devotion to her is not the possession of one local church or one culture—or even one faith community. In today's religious and political climate, this recognition encourages us to make Mary a point of contact with others. One of the little known potential building blocks for interfaith understanding is the fact that both the Christianity and the Muslim faith hold the Virgin Mary in high esteem. The nineteenth chapter of the Qur'an is named for Maryam, the mother of Jesus. Muslims visit Catholic Marian shrines in Europe, and both Christians and Muslims make devotional visits to the Marian shrine at Ephesus near Selçuk, Turkey. An ancient Christian tradition names Ephesus as the place where Mary lived her last years in a house built for her there by the Apostle John.

The Qur'an speaks of Maryam's purity and her devotion and persistence in prayer. (See 3:35–51.) It describes her early life in terms that are very close to the *Protevangelium of James*. She conceives her son, Jesus, through direct intervention by God without male participation. (See 19:22–27.) Jesus, though not divine as in Christian teaching, is a great prophet who is able to do great things because God is with him. Sufism, a form of Islam that encourages direct experience of union with God, honors Mary for her openness to God. There is no tradition of Marian images in Islam because of the prohibition against image making that is intended to protect monotheism. The arts are engaged, however, through poetry. Tim Winter in the list for further reading below offers his readers a lovely sampling of texts, including Muslim poetry expressing devotion to Mary. This shared devotion, if taken up as a subject for dialogue and mutual appreciation, forms an opening in the barriers that have been erected between present-day Islam and Christianity.

MARY'S CONTINUING RELATIONSHIP

Images of Mary, as we have seen, have changed through the ages. Mary gives us comfort in times of sorrow and suffering; strength in our hour of weakness when we desire to make good choices; hope when we look to her for intercession on our behalf. The images represent these and many more roles Mary plays in our lives. Whether she is weeping, holding the child Jesus to her breast, stretching out her arms in a welcoming gesture, or posed as in prayer, her image provides us a safe-haven. In a world in which human power tries to dominate, often the cause of interlocking oppressions, racism, sexism, colonialism, and the threat of ecological disaster, how is Mary imaged in a way that challenges and sustains us, especially for those who have traditionally looked to her for religious sustenance? Her image is ever renewing itself in relationship to the urgent needs in the lives of those devoted to her.

FOR FURTHER READING

Winter, Tim. "Mary in Islam," *Mary: The Complete Resource*. Sarah Jane Boss, ed. New York: Oxford, 2007. A brief introduction to the Virgin Mary in Scripture and devotion in Islam.

Bostwick, Bernadette. http://www.grreenmountainmonastery.org/hand. htm. At this site, Sister Bernadette explains her contemporary icon of Mary of the Cosmos.

Taylor, Sarah McFarland. *Green Sisters: A Spiritual Ecology*. Cambridge: Harvard University Press, 2007. Reports on Taylor's research on Roman Catholic congregations of women religious who live out a particular dedication to the preservation and flourishing of the ecosystem. For some of these groups, devotion to Mary is part of their spirituality.

CHAPTER 6
Prayers

WE FLY TO YOUR PROTECTION

We fly to your protection,
O holy Mother of God;
despise not our petitions
in our necessities,
but deliver us always from all danger,
O glorious and blessed Virgin.
Amen.

HAIL MARY

Hail Mary, full of grace.
The Lord is with thee.
Blessed are thou among women,
and blessed is the fruit of thy womb, Jesus.
Holy Mary, Mother of God,
pray for us sinners,
now and at the hour of our death.
Amen.

MEMORARE

Remember, O most gracious Virgin Mary,
that never was it known
that anyone who fled to your protection,
implored your help, or sought your intercession
was left unaided.
Inspired with this confidence,
I fly to you, O virgin of virgins, my Mother.
To you I come,
before you I stand, sinful and sorrowful.
O Mother of the Word Incarnate,
despise not my petitions,
but in your mercy, hear and answer me.
Amen.

MAGNIFICAT

"My spirit proclaims the greatness of the Lord,
my spirit finds joy in God my savior
For he has looked upon his servant in her lowliness;
all ages to come shall call me blessed.
God who is mighty has done great things for me,
holy is his name;
His mercy is from age to age
on those who fear him.
He has shown might with his arm;
he has confused the proud in their inmost thoughts.

He has deposed the mighty from their thrones
and raised the lowly to high places.
The hungry he has given every good thing;
while the rich he has sent away empty.
He has upheld Israel his servant,
ever mindful of her mercy;
Even as he promised our fathers,
promised Abraham and his descendants forever."

HAIL, HOLY QUEEN

Hail, holy Queen, Mother of Mercy; hail our life,
our sweetness and our hope. To you do we cry,
poor banished children of Eve.
To you do we send up our sighs,
mourning and weeping in this valley of tears.
Turn, then, most gracious advocate,
your eyes of mercy toward us.
And after this our exile show unto us
the blessed fruit of your womb, Jesus,
O clement, O loving, O sweet Virgin Mary.

REGINA COELI

Queen of heaven, rejoice, alleluia.
For he whom you merited to bear, alleluia.
Has risen as he said, alleluia.
Pray for us to God, alleluia.
Rejoice and be glad, O Virgin Mary, alleluia.
Because the Lord is truly risen, alleluia.

Let us pray: O God, who by the Resurrection of your Son,
our Lord Jesus Christ, granted joy to the whole world, grant,
we beg of you, that through the intercession of the Virgin
Mary, his Mother, we may lay hold of the joys of eternal life,
through the same Christ Our Lord. Amen.

AKATHIST HYMN

Hail, O Tabernacle of God the Word;
  hail, Holy One, more holy than the saints.
Hail, O Ark that the spirit has gilded;
  hail, sacred Glory of reverent priests.
Hail, unshakable Tower of the Church;
  hail, unbreakable Wall of the Kingdom.
Hail, O you through whom the trophies are raised.
  hail, O you through whom the enemies are routed.
Hail, O Healing of my body;
  hail, O Salvation of my soul.
Hail, O Bride and Maiden everpure.

REJOICE, MOTHER OF GOD

Rejoice, Mother of God, Virgin Immaculate.
Rejoice, you who received joy from the Angel.
Rejoice, you who conceived the brightness of eternal Light.
Rejoice, Mother.
Rejoice, Holy Mother of God and Virgin.
All creation extols you.
Mother of Light, pray for us.

LITANY OF THE BLESSED VIRGIN MARY (LORETO)

Lord, have mercy. Christ, have mercy.
Lord, have mercy. Christ, hear us.
   Christ, graciously hear us.
God the Father of Heaven, have mercy on us.
God the Son, Redeemer, have mercy on us.
God the Holy Ghost, have mercy on us.
Holy Trinity, one God, have mercy on us.
Holy Mary, pray for us.
Holy mother of God, *pray for us.*
Holy virgin of virgins, *pray for us.*
Mother of Christ, *pray for us.*
Mother of divine grace, *pray for us.*
Mother most pure, *pray for us.*
Mother most chaste, *pray for us.*
Mother inviolate, *pray for us.*
Mother undefiled, *pray for us.*
Mother most amiable, *pray for us.*
Mother most admirable, *pray for us.*
Mother of good counsel, *pray for us.*
Mother of our Creator, *pray for us.*
Mother of our Savior, *pray for us.*
   Virgin most merciful, *pray for us.*
   Virgin most faithful, *pray for us.*
   Mirror of justice, *pray for us.*
   Seat of wisdom, *pray for us.*
   Cause of our joy, *pray for us.*
   Spiritual vessel, *pray for us.*
   Vessel of honor, *pray for us.*

Singular vessel of devotion, *pray for us.*
Mystical rose, *pray for us.*
Tower of David, *pray for us.*
Tower of ivory, *pray for us.*
House of gold, *pray for us.*
Ark of the Covenant, *pray for us.*
Gate of Heaven, *pray for us.*
Morning star, *pray for us.*
Health of the sick, *pray for us.*
Refuge of sinners, *pray for us.*
Comforter of the afflicted, *pray for us.*
Help of Christians, *pray for us.*
Queen of angels, *pray for us.*
Queen of patriarchs, *pray for us.*
Queen of prophets, *pray for us.*
Queen of apostles, *pray for us.*
Queen of martyrs, *pray for us.*
Queen of confessors, *pray for us.*
Queen of virgins, *pray for us.*
Queen of all saints, *pray for us.*
Queen conceived without Original Sin, *pray for us.*
Queen assumed into Heaven, *pray for us.*
Queen of the most holy Rosary, *pray for us.*
Queen of peace, *pray for us.*

Lamb of God, who takest away the sins of the world,
Spare us, O Lord.
Lamb of God, who takest away the sins of the world,
Graciously hear us, O Lord.
Lamb of God, who takest away the sins of the world,
Have mercy on us.

Pray for us, O Holy Mother of God that we may be made
worthy of the promises of Christ.

Let us pray: Grant, we beseech Thee, O Lord God,
that we your servants may enjoy perpetual health
of mind and body and by the glorious intercession
of the Blessed Mary, ever Virgin, be delivered
from present sorrow and enjoy eternal happiness.
Through Christ Our Lord. Amen.

LITANY OF MARY OF NAZARETH (PAX CHRISTI USA)

By Jean Wolbert, OSB, in collaboration with Anne McCarthy, OSB,
and Margaret Wehrer. © Pax Christi USA.

Glory to you, God our Creator...
breathe into us new life, new meaning.
Glory to you, God our Savior...
Lead us in the way of peace and justice.
Glory to you, healing Spirit...
Transform us to empower others.

Mary, wellspring of peace...Be our guide.
Model of strength
Model of gentleness
Model of trust
Model of courage
Model of patience
Model of risk
Model of openness
Model of perseverance

Mother of the liberator...Pray for us.
Mother of the homeless
Mother of the dying
Mother of the nonviolent
Widowed mother
Unwed mother
Mother of a political prisoner
Mother of the condemned

Mother of the executed criminal
Oppressed woman...Lead us to life.
Liberator of the oppressed
Marginalized woman
Comforter of the afflicted
Cause of our joy
Sign of contradiction
Beaker of bondage
Political refugee
Seeker of sanctuary
First disciple
Sharer in Christ's passion
Seeker of God's will
Witness to Christ's resurrection

Woman of mercy...Empower us.
Woman of faith
Woman of contemplation
Woman of vision
Woman of wisdom and understanding
Woman of grace and truth
Woman, pregnant with hope
Woman, centered in God

Closing prayer:
Mary, Queen of Peace, we entrust our lives to you.
Shelter us from war, hatred, and oppression.

Teach us to live in peace, to educate ourselves for peace.
Inspire us to act justly, to revere all God has made.
Root peace firmly in our hearts and in our world. Amen.